HIDDEN IN PLAIN SIGHT

FINDING WISDOM AND MEANING IN THE PARTS OF THE BIBLE MOST PEOPLE SKIP

BOYD SEEVERS

BETHANY HOUSE PUBLISHERS

a division of Baker Publishing Group
Minneapolis, Minnesota

© 2012 by Boyd Seevers

Published by Bethany House Publishers
11400 Hampshire Avenue South
Bloomington, Minnesota 55438
www.bethanyhouse.com

Bethany House Publishers is a division of
Baker Publishing Group, Grand Rapids, Michigan

Printed in the United States of America

Library of Congress Cataloging-in-Publication Data

Seevers, Boyd.
    Hidden in plain sight : finding wisdom and meaning in the parts of the Bible
most people skip / Boyd Seevers.
        p. cm.
    Summary: "A Bible professor shows how readers can learn and grow from
the genealogies, confusing prophecies, and other lesser-known parts of the
Bible"—Provided by publisher.
    Includes bibliographical references and index.
    ISBN 978-0-7642-0872-0 (pbk. : alk. paper) 1. Bible. O.T.—Criticism, inter-
pretation, etc. I. Title. 4870 5494 6/12
BS1171.3.S435 2012
221.6—dc23   2011045022

Occasionally the author uses his own translation to better communicate a particular point that the original language allows.

Cover design by Eric Walljasper

12   13   14   15   16   17   18   7   6   5   4   3   2   1

This book is dedicated to my parents, Vernon and Marlene, who first taught me the value of knowing God's Word,

and to the students at Northwestern College, who share my love of God's Word and are honest enough to admit that it is sometimes hard to understand, and even boring. It is a joy to discuss with them the kinds of issues treated in this book so we can hear God speak through his Word into our world.

HIDDEN
IN PLAIN
SIGHT

Contents

Acknowledgments

This author wishes to thank the following:

- My very capable and kind editor, Andy McGuire, and the rest of the staff at Bethany House. Working with them on this project has been a pleasure.

- A former student, Ruth Page, whose capstone paper at Northwestern College, "The Gospel According to Leviticus," has helped me better understand and appreciate Leviticus, and provided much of the material for the corresponding chapter in this book.

- My friend and colleague Randy Nelson for his insight and help on matters of hermeneutics.

- My very capable and helpful teaching assistant, Elyse Kallgren, for her skilled and prompt editing, and her encouragement.

Introduction

Do you think reading the Bible is tough at times, or even boring? That's okay. You're not alone.

You probably picked up this book because you're having trouble slogging through certain passages of the Bible, finding it difficult to understand them, let alone appreciate them. Maybe the Bible is a fairly new book for you, and you're trying to read it to learn more about God and relate to him better. Good for you!

But perhaps it's not going so well. You find yourself getting bogged down as you keep running into parts of God's Word that you don't understand or that you find really dull. Maybe that leaves you frustrated, a little confused, and thinking, *Why doesn't this work better? Why should it be so hard? Shouldn't God* want *me to read his Word and help me get more out of it? How can it possibly be true that all of God's Word is "profitable," or useful, as it says in 2 Timothy 3:16? Have you* seen *some of the stuff in there?*

If you've ever had questions like these or felt this way, again, it's okay. You're not alone.

On the other hand, maybe you're not so new at this. You have read the Bible a fair bit and gotten a lot out of it—at least most of it. Maybe you have even tried to read all the way through the Bible. Again, good for you!

But still . . .

You keep running into parts of the Bible that are tough to get through. You started well in Genesis and really liked most of it (apart from the genealogies), and the first part of Exodus was enjoyable too. But the description of the Tabernacle in Exodus was kind of dry, and then it was repeated. But you got through that and hoped for something better. Then you found yourself in Leviticus with its laws of clean and unclean animals and such, and who needs all that? Numbers wasn't much better, so you gave up. If you have ever experienced something like this when trying to read through the Bible, that's okay too. You are not alone.

Or maybe you're a seasoned veteran when it comes to reading the Bible. You have known God for a long time and truly love reading his Word. You have read all the way through the Bible numerous times, and can honestly say that you enjoy it—most of it anyway. Good for you! What you'd like is a way to better understand and get more out of certain parts of the Bible. You no longer need an introduction, you need a pick-me-up.

After all, some of the laws in the Old Testament seem irrelevant because of Jesus' ministry. Good point. And those genealogies are real winners—full of *begats* and lots of names you can't pronounce that don't seem to have much to do with anything. And then there are those prophets in the Old Testament or those weird visions in Daniel and Revelation—*What on earth are they talking about?* You're a veteran, but maybe you wouldn't mind a little help dealing with tough sections like these.

So regardless of how much you have read the Bible, if you find parts of it confusing, irrelevant, or dry, know that you're in good company. Many people feel that way. I have multiple degrees in Bible and theology and teach the Bible for a living, yet I still find parts of the Bible a little confusing and yes, even boring at times.

I have even had the pleasure (and known the challenges) of living in Israel for a number of years. I studied in Jerusalem for a year with my wife, and later we lived in Tiberias, Israel, for several more years doing ministry and raising our children there. Israel is a fascinating but difficult place, and of course, it's the location of many of the events in the Bible. Living in the land of the Bible with the people and culture of the Bible (kind of) was a fascinating and worthwhile experience. That background often helps in understanding where the Bible's authors are coming from. But it doesn't always work. Sometimes I still get lost in what they're saying, and I can't always see connections between their world back then and my world here and now.

So What's the Plan?

I teach the Bible at a Christian college, and most of my students get perplexed now and then too. In fact, I'll be including quotes from some of them that express their frustrations with many of the parts of the Bible treated in this book. Because they struggle with the Bible at times, like you probably do, they seem relieved to discover that their professor also thinks some sections of the Bible are challenging and not very exciting. So we talk about why those sections seem that way. We discuss who the original audience was and what their needs were, as well as what the original authors intended to teach or communicate to them. Once the students understand those things, they can better appreciate these sections for what they are, and not try to turn them into something they aren't supposed to be. Then they can see which parts of those passages are applicable today.

It's really a rather liberating process. It helps my students learn more from these sections and relieves some of the guilt from thinking that parts of the inspired Word of God are mundane or irksome. My students seem to appreciate it, and I think you will too.

Would you like some guidance in getting through the tough parts of the Bible? There is hope. This book will walk you through certain challenging parts of the Bible, but it will also give you a strategy for how you can approach similar sections on your own. The key to making the commonplace parts more interesting and helpful comes down to understanding the original context and purpose of a passage and then asking the right questions. *Who wrote this? To whom was it written? What was their situation? What were their needs? What were the author's purposes in saying what he did?*

Once you understand these issues, you can better appreciate the original purpose of the passage. Sometimes that purpose overlaps with our situation today, sometimes not. If it does, that section is more relevant. If it doesn't, the section has less relevance, and we can treat it differently. All Scripture *is* inspired, but not all of it was addressed to the kinds of situations that God's people face here and now. Sorting out the purpose and relevance helps us better understand and appreciate the various sections of the Word of God for what they are.

Once we get a handle on the original context and purpose of a passage, we then go on to its teaching and application. We need to ask what the passage teaches about God's character and nature, or about the world and human nature, or about how God's people should think and act. Then we can apply those truths. Thus, understanding the original context and purpose leads us to a clearer understanding of the teaching, which guides us to what we can apply in our day and in our particular situation.

Do you think this sort of approach would help you? If so, let's begin. We'll start with a short chapter describing this process more thoroughly, laying out our strategy for dealing with these difficult parts of the Bible. Then we'll follow that process with other chapters that tackle some of the most challenging parts of the Bible: the Old Testament law, the sacrifices in Leviticus, genealogies, the division of land in Joshua, the repetition of Kings and Chronicles, negative Ecclesiastes, prophets, and apocalyptic material. We'll conclude with a final chapter summarizing what we have learned, spelling out in easy-to-understand fashion the strategy that you can use when you come to other parts of the Bible that might be baffling or monotonous. All of God's Word is profitable. Let's learn how to enjoy it!

1

What Makes a Passage of Scripture Hard to Understand or Even Boring?

The Problem

As stated in the introduction to this book, the Bible is God's Word, but some parts of it are just plain hard to understand—even boring. Some parts of the Bible are *both* difficult to understand *and* boring. After all, if I can't understand something, I usually lose interest in it pretty quickly.

How can this be? How can God's Word, which is more precious than gold and sweeter than honey (Psalm 19:10), not be clear and relevant to us, God's people?

The answer can be rather simple—often when the Bible is hard to understand, it's because it wasn't originally written for us. Don't get me wrong—the Bible is from God and always will be useful for teaching, rebuking, correcting, and training in righteousness (2 Timothy 3:16). But God didn't originally write it to modern Christians living in the twenty-first century

AD. It was written sometime between two thousand and four thousand years ago to people living on the other side of the world in a very different culture and speaking a very different language than ours. If we read something written for an audience that far removed, of course it can be difficult to understand.

This difference is especially challenging in the parts of the Bible that this book will address: the laws of the Old Testament, the genealogies, many of the prophets, and apocalyptic literature (such as the book of Revelation or the second half of Daniel). Today, we often find ourselves far from the situations addressed by those laws, from the peoples named in the genealogies, from the messages the prophets addressed, and especially from the kind of literature found in Revelation. These parts of the Bible seem distant to us, our world, and our normal methods of communication.

To illustrate the challenge of understanding material written for a different audience, I sometimes show my students a piece of writing they have never seen before and ask them to interpret it. Here's one example:

I will finally write and let you know how the journey went. It was difficult. We left from Gothenburg by boat on the 21st to Fredrikshavn, then by train to Bremen . . . where we waited for two days. Then we went by boat . . . we arrived the 5th of this month . . . We were sick most of the time on the ship. The weather was very bad and stormy. There were 1,058 passengers, about two hundred Swedes at the most. Three babies were born, two (people) died and one fell overboard. We had several people from Hestra for company but they continued toward Minnesota.

I have my students read such a passage without introduction, and then ask them to interpret it. Often they do a good job. They guess it was a letter or journal written by someone from Sweden traveling to Minnesota in the late 1800s or early 1900s. And they're mostly correct. The excerpt above is from a letter written by Joshua Anderson, my wife's Swedish great-grandfather, describing to his father back in rural, south-central Sweden how the journey to America went for him and his brother. In 1879, Joshua and August Anderson left Sweden, traveled by train and boat to Germany, then by steamship to New York City. Finally, they traveled overland to Clermont, Pennsylvania, to live with their older brother John, who had immigrated a few years earlier, and to work with him in the coal mines there.

I have to explain this contextual information to my students because the letter wasn't originally written to them, and much of it would not be obvious to a modern reader. Joshua Anderson's father wouldn't have needed any explanation about the context, of course, because he would have known it firsthand. He also would have perfectly understood the letter in its original Swedish, whereas my students and I need to use the copy translated into English. Joshua's father was personally connected to the situation—he knew many of the people referred to in the letter, and he would have known about most of the places mentioned as well. He *was* the original audience, so he probably didn't find the letter difficult to understand, and it wouldn't be boring to him at all. In fact, he probably found the letter very interesting, because he surely cared deeply about how his two sons had fared on their long, difficult journey to their new homeland.

Like my students, you probably wouldn't know the background information of such an excerpt, and though you would understand the facts as I just described them, without a personal connection to the people or places mentioned in a letter, you might well lose interest.

So it can be with the Bible. Where we might understand something of a letter written a century ago that describes a journey to America, by contrast, the Bible was written *thousands* of years ago, *much* farther away. It speaks of people and places we may know little or nothing about and may describe experiences that seem light-years removed from our world. For these reasons, we may see little connection between ourselves and what the Bible is saying.

The Reason for the Problem

Why would God allow people like us—who want to understand his Word—to have difficulty with it? Why not just communicate to us in a way that does away with all these barriers of time and distance and language and culture, and speak clearly to us?

When I first began to comprehend these barriers that make the Bible more difficult to understand, the situation honestly annoyed me. Parts like the Old Testament's laws, genealogies, prophets, and apocalyptic visions seemed needlessly difficult. Surely God could have done better, I thought. But the more I have considered the way God has chosen to act and communicate in and to our world, the more I appreciate the way he did it—even with the built-in barriers and challenging parts of the Bible.

God did *not* intentionally communicate in a manner detached from our world. He could have avoided the barriers, but apparently thought it better to communicate as he did. He didn't drop a book from heaven that began with "Listen up! Know that I, God, am eternal, all-powerful, and infinitely good. Trust me, and do what I tell you. Now, get on with it." While such a style may have been clearer and easier to understand in some ways, God chose to communicate differently.

God decided to show us what he is like and what he wants from us by giving us a book that records *his interactions with earlier peoples.* His book isn't divorced from time and context; it's imbedded in them. He dealt with real people, in real places, who faced real problems, and he helped them wrestle through their issues. I like that.

I like that my God is *really* involved with the kinds of issues that I face in my world, at least in general. The Bible doesn't talk about cars and the Internet and other things important in my world, but it has plenty to say about relationships and faith and trusting God even when we don't understand why he allows some things to work out as he does. Those things are timeless, even if cars and the Internet are not. God knows what I face and has dealt with it before. His book isn't a detached theological treatise. It's a record of a God communicating and acting *in history,* and later even *coming into history himself,* to show us what he's like and to teach us how to relate to him. He wasn't afraid to get his hands dirty. I like that.

Unfortunately, this more real and more personal method of communicating also means that gaps develop over time. The further we are removed chronologically, geographically, linguistically, and culturally from what God originally said and did, the more challenging it becomes to understand the Bible. We serve a God who spoke and acted in real situations, but we have to overcome the gaps of time and space, language and culture, to fully grasp what he told us. Doing that helps us to better appreciate it. The stories in the Bible become more real, and God's involvement is more personal than if we read a list of timeless, detached truths.

The Solution to the Problem

So how do we overcome the gaps between our world and the world in which God originally spoke and acted so we can understand what he has said?

When you reach the point of asking such a question, you have already taken the first step—realizing such gaps exist. Many people do not understand this. They try to read the Bible as though it were written to people today. Sometimes that works, because sometimes the overlap between the two worlds is strong enough to make an immediate and wholesale transfer of the commands and principles found in a particular section of Scripture.

However, when the connection between the biblical world and our own is *not* so obvious, we have more work to do. We have to cross the gaps to understand the text more like the original audience did. We have to do more than make the relatively short leap to the world of a Swedish immigrant; we have to jump much farther back to the people living in the Greco-Roman world of the New Testament, or the Middle Eastern world of the Old Testament.

We can never fully succeed in bridging that gap, of course. Just as we can never completely understand *everything* that Joshua Anderson told his father in his letter or fully appreciate what his father thought or felt as he read his son's letter, neither can we fully understand the perspective of the Israelites and early Christians when they received the biblical texts. But we can try. We can typically learn enough of the original context to know who was saying what to whom, and what the main issues were. The better we learn these things, the better we will be able to understand the difficult parts of the Bible and appreciate the things hidden there in plain sight.

What things do we need to learn? First of all, we need to do the best we can at grasping the *original context* of the material we are reading. Once we know the original context, we must figure out the *kind of literature* we're dealing with and how to best interpret it. Some texts are easy to recognize and interpret (like stories), but others are more difficult (like apocalyptic visions). Finally, we need to sort out what *application* the original commands or teachings imply, even in our very different world. Let's examine these in more detail.

1. What is the original context?

One reason the Bible is often so challenging is that we don't know the world from which it came. To help sort this out, I find it helpful to ask the questions *Who? What? When? Where? Why?* And finally, *How?*

WHO—WAS THE AUTHOR?

I start by asking *Who wrote this? Who was the original author? What do we know about him?* (Most ancient cultures were dominated by males—including the cultures from which came the biblical books. That may not necessarily have been right, but it's the way it was. Although we don't know who wrote all the books of the Bible, the authors that we have been able to identify were males.) Sometimes we know little about the author, other times we know a great deal. *What we know about an author helps us better understand what he wrote.* For example, the apostle Paul wrote the letter to the Philippians. We know a great deal about Paul, the city of Philippi, and Paul's ministry there, and this information is helpful in interpreting and applying that letter.

Occasionally we *don't* know who wrote a particular book of the Bible. If we don't, what *do* we know or what can we tell about him? For example, we don't know for sure who wrote the book of Joshua. Some things in the book point to Joshua or another participant in the conquest of Canaan; other things point to someone years later. Regardless, we can see that much of the material came from the time of the conquest and reflects what God said and did at that key time in the history of Israel. Whoever wrote it wanted the Israelites after the conquest to realize that God had kept his earlier promises to their forefathers and given them the Promised Land. God had been faithful to the Israelites; they should be faithful to God so they could continue to enjoy living in the Promised Land. This is clear even if we don't know the identity of the author of the whole book.

You may be asking where to get information such as the identity of the author. Occasionally a book of the Bible will start by naming the author (Romans 1:1), but usually not. If the identity of the author isn't obvious, the place to find such information as well as other information addressed in the following paragraphs is in a study Bible or a Bible dictionary. Many good study Bibles are available today, and most of them contain one to three pages of introductory material that address these very issues. Bible dictionaries or encyclopedias also have articles on the books of the Bible that explain their context and content. It's a good idea to buy a study Bible or other source and get into the habit of reading the introduction first. It will give you the big picture of what the book is about as well as answer questions about authorship and original recipients.

WHO—WERE THE ORIGINAL RECIPIENTS?

To whom was the author writing? What do we know about them? What was their situation? How can their identity and situation help us understand what is written in the book and apply it in our time? As before, we may or may not know this information fully, but determining it as much as possible will help clarify the meaning.

WHAT—WAS THE AUTHOR COMMUNICATING TO HIS AUDIENCE?

What are the main issues the author addresses? What are the big ideas in the book? This addresses the core of a book's message. It's easy to lose sight of the forest when you're examining the trees. Starting out with a book's main ideas in mind should help us keep from getting lost in the details as we make our way through.

WHEN—DID THE EVENTS OCCUR, AND WHEN WAS THE BOOK WRITTEN?

If the book records events, do we know when they happened and in what context? If the book is something like a letter or piece of poetry, do we know when it was written? What else do we know that would help set the context for the material? Sometimes the events and writing took place close to the same time (like Paul writing to the churches he had just visited), but other times there's a great gap between the events and the writing (Genesis tells of the creation of the world, but Moses wasn't around at the time; he only wrote about it much later). If there is such a gap, *how does the later time and perspective affect the interpretation of the earlier events?*

WHERE—DID THE EVENTS OCCUR, AND WHERE WAS IT WRITTEN?

Similar to the previous issue, the location may be important for understanding the text, and the original events and the writing about them may not have occurred in the same place.

WHY—WAS THIS AUTHOR WRITING THIS TO THIS AUDIENCE?

What was the author's goal? What outcome or response did he wish from the readers of his writing? Occasionally an author will give us a clear statement of purpose (as in 1 John 5:13), but usually we will have to infer his purpose(s) from what he has written. Either way, keeping the apparent purpose in mind helps us interpret what the author said and why.

HOW—DID THE AUTHOR WRITE WHAT HE DID?

This often goes back to the issue of the type of literature used. *Is the material historical narrative? Poetry? Philosophical musing? Prophetic proclamation? Apocalyptic vision?* Knowing the type of literature used often provides enormous help in comprehending what is being said. Some types of literature are easy to recognize and interpret, while others are quite challenging. We will address this issue in the next section as well as in subsequent chapters as we work to sort out what is being said and taught in the more challenging parts of the Bible.

2. What type of literature are we reading, and are we interpreting it in the right way?

As noted above, recognizing and interpreting the *genre* or type of literature used is often the key to understanding and applying it properly. I have found that students need to go through two steps to handle different types of literature properly.

The first step is to realize that the Bible *does use* different types of literature. Although we intuitively know and naturally deal with various types of communication (news reports, personal conversations, songs), we may not realize that the Bible contains a similar variety. It contains history, poetry, philosophy, sermons, letters, legal material, and so on, and some of these have specific guidelines we need to follow in order to interpret them properly. We can interpret some types of biblical literature rather intuitively (historical narrative, the Psalms), so we might not think much about it. But other types are more difficult (covenants, proverbs, apocalyptic prophecy) and we need to take care to understand them rightly. If we don't, we can get ourselves quite lost or off track. So first we need to recognize that the Bible incorporates various types of literature.

Second, we need to recognize *what kind* of literature a particular section is and use the proper guidelines for interpreting it. Some are fairly easy; others can be quite difficult. We will look into the genre or type of literature for each section of the Bible that we examine in the subsequent chapters of this book.

3. How should we respond to the commands or principles contained in a passage?

Finally, after we learn about the context and understand the kind of literature we are reading, we also need to sort out from a particular section what is relevant for our day and how we can apply it, if at all. Not all the Bible was equally relevant even for the original audience, so neither will it be for us today. For example, the second half of the book of Joshua is mostly a description of the'boundaries for the areas of land allotted to the various Israelite tribes. That information would have been important when settling into their lands, and critical when disputes arose, which almost certainly occurred. But those border descriptions probably didn't help the majority of Israelites in their daily lives as they struggled with relating properly to one another and to their God. The Psalms, the Proverbs, and even the laws in Deuteronomy probably served them better on a daily basis.

The same would be even truer now. The distance between our world and that of the original audience means that some parts of the Bible are less relevant to us. All Scripture is inspired by God and profitable to believers today (2 Timothy 3:16), but not all of it is equally useful, especially when compared to its benefit for the first audience. The divisions of land in the book of Joshua present a good example. Since we don't live in those areas, the descriptions of the borders between tribes mean almost nothing to us, and the original readers may have needed the information only occasionally. Perhaps the best we can do with passages like this is to appreciate how they would have benefitted the original audience.

Fortunately, the Bible doesn't have too many sections with such limited value to today's reader. Usually there is some relevance to the modern believer to one degree or another. As we make our way through the chapters of this book, we will examine each section (Old Testament law, genealogies, etc.) to learn its context, genre, and relevance for the original audience as well as for believers today. Even when the section doesn't have direct application for us, we can often see principles or illustrations of God's character that help us better understand him or how to relate to him.

Study Questions

1. What parts of the Bible have you found hardest to understand or boring? Why these parts?

2. How much have you been aware of the gaps in time, distance, language, and culture between our world and the original text of the Bible?

3. Have you found a Bible study tool to help you bridge the gaps between our world and the biblical world—such as the introductions to each book in a study Bible, or some other resource like a Bible dictionary or Bible encyclopedia? If you have, what tool works best for you, and why?

4. If you aren't already doing so, can you figure out a way to discern the original context: Who (were the original author and audience)? What (are the main themes the author sought to communicate to his audience)? When and where (did the events occur, and was the book written)? Why and how (did this author write to this audience)?

5. Do you think about the different types of literature in the Bible, and are you aware of how to interpret the various genres differently? Which do you find most difficult?

6. Do you think it's okay to assume some parts of the Bible were more important for their original audience than for us? If so, which would be more important today and which less important? (For example—would the sections dealing with things like the sacrificial system before Jesus be less applicable to Christians today?)

2

Learning From Old Testament Law

The Problem: Why Are Some of the Laws of the Old Testament So Hard to Understand and Appreciate?

Most people who read through the Old Testament come to the sections of laws that God gave to ancient Israel and find many of them incomprehensible. For example, when I asked my students what they considered to be the least understandable part of the Bible, a student named Allison wrote, "The Old Testament laws. I am bored and confused by modern legal material; ancient legal material is even worse." When I read her comment, I thought, *Amen*. Trying to wade through the instructions for doing my yearly taxes is painful at best. Trying to read other types of legal material is usually worse. So maybe it's not so surprising that legal material from an ancient society like biblical Israel can be challenging.

Conversely, I do find some of the laws in the Bible intriguing. For example, Moses instructed parents to deal with rebellious sons as follows: "If someone has a stubborn and rebellious son who does not obey his father and mother and will not listen to them when they discipline him, his father and mother shall take hold of him and bring him to the elders [officials] at the gate of his town. . . . Then all the men of his town are to stone him to death. . . . All Israel will hear of it and be afraid" (Deuteronomy 21:18–21). *Stone a rebellious child?* It seems that parents would have to be at the end of their rope to subject a son to such a fate. But it wouldn't take too many such cases in a generation to motivate other children who heard of it to be obedient. I'm just glad we didn't have that law around when I was a teenager!

Many of the laws in the Old Testament are even more challenging to understand and appreciate. Take this law directed toward Israelite homeowners: "When you build a new house, make a parapet [a low, protective wall] around your roof so that you may not bring the guilt of bloodshed on your house if someone falls from the roof" (Deuteronomy 22:8). I understand that we need to keep people safe, but for many years I wondered about requiring people to build a "fence" around their roof. Many roofs are too steep to climb on, and even if they're not, why would people be on someone else's roof? Why would God give Israel such a law?

I didn't understand the law for a long time, but during the years our family lived in Israel I learned to appreciate it. Even today, many people in that part of the world build homes with flat roofs (and low protective walls) to provide more living space. Roofs make a great place to hang out the wash, sit and relax in the evening, and sleep during the summer in the cool, fresh air, when houses are still warm from the day's sun. When our kids were small and we lived in a home with a flat roof, we would sometimes send them up on the roof to play. The roof was easy to get to from inside, wasn't muddy, and since it had a good protecting wall, it was safe. Our oldest daughter even learned to ride her bike on the roof! Thus we quickly experienced the need for a good protecting wall to keep people safe on the roof in that part of the world.

Having lived for a time in the world of the Bible has helped me to better understand some of the Old Testament laws, but I still find many that defy explanation or application. For example, "Do not cook a young goat in its mother's milk." Really? Why not? God apparently thought this law important enough to repeat it three times (Exodus 23:19; 34:26; Deuteronomy 14:21), but *why* this was important still escapes me. I don't worry about that particular law too much, though, because I rarely eat young goats or cook with goat's milk. I think more about other biblical laws, like the one forbidding tattoos. Tattoos seem more relevant than goat's milk, and since many people in my culture have tattoos, my students ask about this law (and more than once I have considered getting a tattoo). So when I read, "Do not . . . put tattoo marks on yourselves. I am the Lord" (Leviticus 19:28), I wonder why God prohibited them, and I especially wonder if believers today should avoid them.

So what do we do with such laws in the Old Testament? How can we better understand and appreciate them? And perhaps most important, how can we know which ones we should follow, and which, if any, we can assume are no longer applicable? I suggest we tackle these important matters by asking and answering the following questions: *What purpose(s) did these laws originally serve? What did they teach their original audience?* And finally, *what can we learn from them and which still apply today?* These are important issues for modern Christians who are struggling to understand and properly relate to the Bible. So let's get started.

The Point—What Purposes Did the Laws Originally Serve?

Before we can address the original purpose for the laws of the Old Testament, we need to define the term *law*. It can and does mean a number of different things related to the Old Testament, so let's narrow the discussion a bit.

What do we mean by law?

The Bible uses the word *law* in at least five different ways, the last two of which are most applicable to our discussion. These five proper but different uses of the term are as follows:

1. *The Pentateuch (the first five books of the Bible).* Jesus told his followers that he did not "come to abolish *the Law* or the Prophets" since not even the smallest part "will by any means disappear from *the Law* until everything is accomplished" (Matthew 5:17–18). Here Jesus uses *Law* and *Prophets* to mean two of the three sections of the Jewish Bible (which we call the Old Testament). Jesus was saying that he didn't intend to replace the Old Testament, but would give full meaning to it through his ministry. Here Jesus uses *Law* for *the first section of the Bible,* made up of the books of Genesis, Exodus, Leviticus, Numbers, and Deuteronomy. That section does contain the kinds of laws we want to address here, but this use is broader than what we will focus on. We don't need to deal with everything in the first five books, only the laws they contain.

2. *The entire Old Testament.* The laws of the Old Testament were so important that people in the New Testament occasionally referred to *the whole Old Testament* by using the term *Law*. For example, in John 10:34, Jesus quotes from Psalm 82:6 by saying, "Is it not written in *your Law* . . . ?" Likewise, in 1 Corinthians 14:21, Paul says, "In *the Law* it is written . . ." and then quotes Isaiah 28:11–12. Jesus and Paul are quoting from the Old Testament outside of the Pentateuch, but they still call it "the Law." Apparently they mean the entire Old Testament. Once again, referring to the whole Old Testament as "the Law" would include the laws we want to address in this chapter, but is broader than what we want to focus on now.

3. *A single law or group of laws on a subject.* In Numbers 19:14, God introduces a rule regulating one aspect of ceremonial uncleanness with the expression, "This is *the law* that applies [in the following situation]." Here he clearly means *one specific law.* We find a similar but broader use in Numbers 6:13 and 6:21, referring to a series of laws (in 6:1–21) about a different aspect of a somewhat related subject—the vow of a person the Bible calls a *Nazirite,* a person set apart for service to God in a particular way. In this case, *law* means *a series of rules about a single subject.* These two uses of *law* do include the kinds of laws from the Old Testament that we want to discuss, although we want to discuss (almost) all of them as a group, so this use is too narrow.

4. *A general term for all of God's laws.* In Deuteronomy 4:8, Moses asks the nation of Israel a rhetorical question that emphasizes the greatness of the rules that guided their relationship with their God: "And what other nation . . . [has] such righteous decrees and judgments as *this body of*

laws . . . ?" Here *law* refers to *the entire code of laws* given by God, and almost exactly matches the perspective of the term we wish to address in this chapter. It speaks about all the laws of the Old Testament as a group. Most laws in the Old Testament were part of the Mosaic Covenant (see below), but this grouping would include a few more—such as the laws we find in Genesis before we get to the Mosaic Covenant in the book of Exodus.

5. The Mosaic Covenant—Israel's national covenant with God. When Moses led the Israelites out of Egypt at the beginning of the book of Exodus, they went to Mount Sinai and made a national covenant with God, which modern writers often call the Mosaic Covenant (because Moses served as the mediator between God and Israel). Sometimes writers also call it the Sinaitic Covenant (because God made the covenant with Israel at Mount Sinai). The nation of Israel swore to keep this covenant, and the rest of the Old Testament records how well they did or did not do that and what blessings or curses resulted from their loyalty or lack thereof.

This Mosaic Covenant includes the laws we have been discussing and will continue to discuss in this chapter. These laws include general rules such as the Ten Commandments as well as the many more specific laws that follow it, such as not boiling a young goat in its mother's milk. These laws as a group formed the backbone for both Israel's religious practice and their society in general, and were so important that we find them stated twice in the Pentateuch—first in the book of Exodus, and then again in the book of Deuteronomy. God gave these laws to the generation of Israelites that came out of Egypt, and again forty years later to the next generation when they reconfirmed their commitment to the covenant before entering the Promised Land. God thus refers to this national covenant and the laws it contains with the term *the law* (Exodus 24:12) or *this law* (Deuteronomy 31:9). Like the fourth option, this use of *law* works well for our current discussion. We want to talk about all the laws that God gave to Israel, which are expressed in the national covenant he made with them.

What purposes did these laws serve?

These last two uses of *law* define the term as we wish to discuss it in the rest of this chapter. The laws of the Old Testament that puzzle modern Christians are those given by God to the nation of Israel to guide their religion and their society, and usually are spelled out in the great national covenant recorded in the books of Exodus and Deuteronomy. They help form the framework of the covenant between God and the nation of Israel. Thus the laws were God's instructions for the Israelites, explaining how they should relate to God and to one another.

What else can we learn about his purposes in giving the laws? Are the laws negative? Was God trying to be mean, using laws to limit the Israelites' freedom and fun? Indeed, some think of God as a cosmic killjoy, watching for anything that humans might enjoy so he can make a rule against it. Is this what is behind God's laws? Is he playing the part of the big meanie in the sky, waiting to whack us with a celestial stick whenever we get out of line? *Of course not.*

GOD USES LAWS TO PROTECT

Rather than a great limiter of fun, the Bible portrays God as a *provider* and *protector*. God is a generous *provider* who must also act with authority to keep us away from things and behaviors that will harm us. We see this from the earliest parts of the Bible. After creating Adam and placing him in a beautiful garden, God said, "From any tree in the garden you may freely eat;" (Note the generosity and freedom) "but you must not eat from [one particular tree], for when you eat from it you will certainly die" (Genesis 2:16–17, author's translation). (Note how the prohibition *protects* Adam from death.) God is a generous God who also knows that he must protect us from harm, and he makes rules to accomplish that. Unfortunately, we often can't see, or lose sight of, the protective aspect of God's laws and feel he is just keeping us from something we want.

The ancient Israelites probably felt the same way. They knew God was a generous provider. He had created the human race, chosen Israel, and then made them numerous enough to form a nation. When they ended up as slaves in Egypt, he provided freedom for them as well, and promised to take them to a land that he would give to them as a national home. That's a lot of provision. Along with these things, he also gave them rules to live by, largely to protect them from the harm they could do to themselves. He had *provided* for them generously and then acted to *protect* them with rules through the laws imbedded in their national covenant.

GOD USES LAWS TO INSTRUCT

In addition we can see that God used laws as a way of *instructing* the Israelites. One of the common Hebrew terms for law is *Torah,* and its root meaning is "instruction." The Israelites who came out of Egypt needed to form a cohesive society and religion, and God used laws, in part, to instruct them on how to relate to one another and to him in regard to many facets of life. These laws served several different purposes, including giving information, expressing commands, and providing guidance, as discussed below.

The Original Goal—What Did These Laws Teach Israel?

Some laws communicated information

Some laws were primarily *informational,* such as telling the Israelites what God had promised to do for them: "If you pay attention to these laws and are careful to follow them, then the Lord . . . will love you and bless you and increase your numbers" (Deuteronomy 7:12–13). These informational laws told them how they could be blessed, and often provided the basis for obeying other commands, including the motivation to remain faithful to the covenant.

Some laws gave commands

In addition to those that communicated information, many of Israel's laws also *gave commands* that the Israelites needed to obey. Sometimes these commands were expressed in a general, timeless manner, like "Remember the Sabbath day by keeping it holy" (Exodus 20:8), implying that the Israelites should always do this. This law is one of the Ten Commandments, perhaps the best known commands in the Old Testament. They are expressed in this form. Other such general commands may not be as well known, but were timeless and binding as well. For example, "Love the Lord your God and keep his requirements, his decrees, his laws and his commands always" (Deuteronomy 11:1). If you are like me, such commands are the type you typically think of when you think about laws. Indeed, the Old Testament contains many such timeless, general commands, but it also has other laws that were more limited.

Some laws provided guidance

In addition to laws that gave information and expressed commands, other laws *provided guidance* on how to handle specific situations. This type of law was less general and more specific than the timeless laws like the Ten Commandments. Often this form was expressed using "If . . . then . . ." statements. If X occurs, then you must do Y. For example, "*If* you hear . . . that troublemakers have arisen among you and have led the people of their town astray, saying, 'Let us go and worship other gods' . . . *then* you must . . . investigate it thoroughly. And if it is true . . . you must certainly put to the sword [the guilty]" (Deuteronomy 13:12–15). The Israelites weren't commanded to do Y all the time, but only when X was the case.

The laws helped Israelite society function smoothly

So what did these timeless and specific laws of the Old Testament teach? God used them to communicate information, express commands, and provide guidance for the Israelites as they sought to establish their nation and set up a working society. He wasn't trying to stop their fun, but rather help them function well as individuals, in their families, and as a society.

These concepts all show that the laws were intended for positive purposes, but they also show that the laws of the Old Testament were intended for the people of Israel, at least originally. God gave those laws to those people at that time. Thus we can assume they understood the laws rather well. They probably even knew why God told them not to boil a young goat in its mother's milk.

But that was then, and we live now. What kind of perspective should we have about the laws of the Old Testament today? Since the people of Israel were God's people then and we are God's people now, should we relate to those laws just as they did? If not, should we disregard them all as outdated, especially in light of the ministry of Jesus? Or should we keep some and discard others? If the last option is correct, how can we know which to keep and which to discard? These are the questions we want to tackle in the final section of this chapter.

The Benefit—What Can We Learn From, and How Should We Relate to, the Laws in the Old Testament?

So what can we learn from these laws in the Old Testament? And how should modern believers relate to them? As we have already seen, we can begin by appreciating the positive aspects the laws had for their original audience. But after that, what do we do with them? When we read through our Bibles, do we just read them as a somewhat interesting window into an ancient world, with little or no relevance today? Do we still try to follow all or some of them? I wondered about these questions for many years, and have been somewhat surprised to learn the range of views that serious believers have on this subject. I have learned at least five different perspectives modern believers use to relate to the laws of the Old Testament, all of which are helpful to some degree. I summarize those views as follows:

41

1. *All the Old Testament laws still apply, unless specifically cancelled in the New Testament.*

I first heard this perspective from someone I sat next to on an airplane. I often pray for opportunities to talk about my faith with people I have contact with, such as strangers on a plane, but don't always get the opportunity. If I'm able to strike up a conversation and the person asks what I do for a living, I have found that saying "I'm a professor who teaches courses about the Bible" sometimes kills conversation. Some people seem to want to avoid the subject altogether, but others are interested and want to discuss Scripture. On one flight, I sat next to a gentleman who fit the latter. He wanted to talk about the Bible, and the conversation turned to how modern Christians should relate to the Old Testament. I shared some of my perspective, but he clearly thought that all the Old Testament laws were still in effect today, unless something in the New Testament had replaced or cancelled them. Interesting idea with much to commend it, but in the end it seems impractical to me.

I do see a number of reasons that people hold this position. For one, since "[God] is the same yesterday and today and forever" (Hebrews 13:8), couldn't his law be timeless as well? Matthew 24:35 says his Word "will never pass away." If so, how could it no longer be valid? And finally, since God gave his law to his people in the Old Testament, and we are God's people today, wouldn't it apply to us as well? These are good points, and seem true at least to some degree.

On the other hand, the Bible seems to show that some of these points aren't entirely true. God may *be* the same yesterday, today, and forever, but that doesn't mean he *does* the same things all through history. For example, the Bible shows that in the beginning God created the world. But he didn't keep on creating it; he went on and did other things. And the Bible says that one day God will end the world. God's actions change. Perhaps this could apply to his laws as well.

In addition, the Bible makes it quite clear that Jesus' ministry brought about a major change for at least part of the Old Testament laws. Jesus fulfilled the Old Testament law (Matthew 5:17) and brought to it an end (Romans 10:4) in some fashion. Jesus' sacrifice of himself ended the need for us to sacrifice animals to cover our sins before God. This proves that at least some laws in the Old Testament are now outdated. But how can we know if other laws might still be in effect, and if so, which ones?

2. Divide the Old Testament laws into religious, civil, and moral categories, and keep using the moral.

Some find it helpful to group the laws of the Old Testament by their function, organized according to *religious, civil,* and *moral* categories, and consider only the moral laws as still valid. Again, this strategy seems helpful to some degree. Some of the Old Testament laws had a clearly religious function (like the laws in Leviticus 1–7 pertaining to sacrifices), and others were civil, helping Israelite society to function properly (like the instructions for kings in Deuteronomy 17:14–20). Now, since the religious laws changed drastically after the ministry of Jesus and we no longer live under the Israelite monarchy, we can probably assume that these two categories of laws are no longer valid for modern believers, though they probably contain some useful principles (more on that later).

The third of these categories focuses on the laws that deal with moral matters, and thus are more likely to still be valid today. The Ten Commandments would probably fit into this category. The commands to honor God and parents, and prohibiting murder, adultery, theft, and so on seem timeless and valid for all cultures. If religious and civil laws are outdated but moral laws aren't, have we then found the best way to treat Old Testament laws? Should we set aside but still learn from religious and civil laws, yet follow the moral ones? Perhaps.

Though this principle is often very helpful, it too has its weaknesses. For one thing, the three categories of *religious, civil,* and *moral* laws may not be as easily distinguished as they first appear. The Bible doesn't seem to use or recognize distinctions between religious, civil, and moral matters; rather, the Bible seems to assume that God's standards should pervade all of life, and obeying all laws was ultimately an act of obedience to him. So if the Bible doesn't use those three categories, should we? Perhaps not.

In addition, these three categories are hard to define in many cases. Some laws fit easily into one category or the other, but many do not. For example, how would we classify the laws about Israel's king referred to earlier? Clearly the laws for the king serve a civil function, guiding the king to rule the nation well. But they also have a moral imperative for the king, since he was to make a copy of God's law (perhaps intending the term *law* as the Pentateuch [definition #1] or the national covenant [#5]). If the king copied the law for himself, he should have been more apt to obey what God had commanded. Doesn't this make it moral as well as civil? Cases like this seem to suggest a weakness of this approach to the Old Testament laws. It is helpful in many ways and recognizes that some Old Testament laws are no longer binding while others are timeless. But the organizational principle sometimes breaks down and suggests that a different approach might serve us better.

3. Keep using the Ten Commandments. Dismiss the civil and ceremonial laws, and understand the sacrificial laws as setting the stage for Jesus' ministry.

This option is quite close to #2, but is more concrete. It states outright what option #2 implies. It says that the Ten Commandments are still valid. It also understands that the laws pertaining to the nation of Israel and the religious customs before Jesus have been superseded by Jesus' ministry, making them invalid. Even though the laws about sacrifices are not applicable to modern believers, they are quite helpful because they teach us the meaning of sacrifice and lead us to a greater appreciation of what Jesus did. These are all good points.

So this approach is commendable, but also has weaknesses. Since it closely resembles option #2, it shares the weaknesses described earlier. In addition, one can argue that not all the Ten Commandments are still valid. Specifically, the commandment to observe the Sabbath day has been changed to some degree at least by the time of the later New Testament. In the gospels we find the Sabbath discussed much like in the Old Testament—Jews were to rest on the seventh day, and Jesus' opponents accused him of not doing that. But by the time of Paul's letters and the book of Hebrews, for example, the Jewish authors of these books reflect a new understanding of the concept of Sabbath. Believers could legitimately follow different understandings of the Sabbath (Colossians 2:16), and our true Sabbath-rest now comes through faith in Jesus (Hebrews 4:1–11) rather than simply ceasing from work every seventh day. Thus the New Testament seems to alter this commandment, at least in part, perhaps weakening the apparent effectiveness of option #3.

4. Look for the moral principles in the laws of the Old Testament.

Perhaps due to problems like those discussed with the earlier three options, position #4 takes a much more general approach to the issue of how to relate to the laws of the Old Testament. It proposes observing the moral principle in any of the laws, no matter what kind of law it is. From this perspective, a religious law about sacrifices has moral value because it teaches us not only what God required from the Israelites, but what Jesus accomplished through his death. A civil law has moral value because it teaches us how we should conduct ourselves to have an orderly society. And finally, a law about moral behavior obviously shows what God expects from our actions.

This perspective is helpful, as it enables us to learn from any sort of law in the Old Testament. Its weakness lies in how it tends to treat all laws the same, and how it skips the important matter of modern applicability. Surely we can learn from all the laws (or at least most of them), but are some not more beneficial for us to study? In addition, should modern believers still be following any of these laws? If so, which ones? Position #4 doesn't address these important questions very well, suggesting that another position may be more helpful. Perhaps our last one fits the bill.

5. Only the laws repeated in the New Covenant are applicable for modern believers.

Earlier we noted that the laws of the Old Testament helped form much of the structure for the national covenant that God made with Israel at Mount Sinai, which we call the Mosaic Covenant. Perspective #5 uses this and other biblical covenants as the basis for understanding the relationship between God and his people, including the laws that express much of what God expects of us. God's relationship with his people has changed over time, with some similarities and some differences during each period. If the various covenants can provide a helpful framework for understanding that changing relationship and the associated laws, they may help us sort out which laws from the Old Testament, if any, are still applicable.

Before dealing with the Mosaic Covenant and its laws, let's discuss further the various biblical covenants and their relationship to each other. Though parts of this discussion can be debated to some degree, we can see at least five inter-related covenants in the Bible, culminating in the New Covenant. What are these five covenants? From the beginning of the Bible, some would understand God's commands to Adam as a sixth covenant, though the Bible doesn't use the term *covenant* to describe God's relationship to Adam. *Covenant* first appears in the Bible when God promised Noah and his descendants that God would never again destroy the earth with a flood (Genesis 9:1–17). This is what we will consider the first biblical covenant, and it included God's unilateral promise to avoid such an act of judgment in the future.

The second, third, and fourth biblical covenants also come from the Old Testament, and focus primarily on the people and nation of Israel. God made a covenant with Abraham (Genesis 15, 17) and repeated it to the subsequent generations, in which he promised to make Abraham's descendants (the Jewish people) numerous and eventually give them the land of Canaan. God followed through and gave them that land at the time of the Mosaic Covenant, the third covenant, which we have already discussed. In the Mosaic Covenant, God promised to bless Israel and let them enjoy the land as long as they remained faithful to the Mosaic Covenant. If they did not, God said he would send them from the land into exile. God followed through with that promise as well, but long before that, he had also made a covenant with David, Israel's greatest king. In the Davidic Covenant (2 Samuel 7), God had promised David that he would be the first of a line of kings that would rule in Jerusalem, and this line continued until God exiled Israel for breaking the Mosaic Covenant. Thus we see that these covenants were interrelated and linked to God's ongoing relationship with the people of Israel, including some ways their relationship changed over time.

The last of the five biblical covenants grew out of the Mosaic Covenant and culminated with the ministry of Jesus. Toward the end of the Old Testament, when Israel had irrevocably broken the Mosaic Covenant and God was about to expel them from their land, the prophet Jeremiah announced that God would eventually replace the Mosaic Covenant with a "new covenant" (Jeremiah 31:31) that would include an internal motivation to follow God. In Luke 22:20, we see that Jesus inaugurated this covenant with his followers. The later New Testament then uses the New Covenant as the framework for the new relationship that God's people would have with him from that time onward. The author of Hebrews makes it clear that the New Covenant is superior to the Mosaic Covenant that it replaced (Hebrews 8:6–13). We as God's people today are under the New Covenant and enter into relationship with God through faith in his son, Jesus.

Understanding this covenantal framework may well help us to better understand the laws of the Old Testament and how we should relate to them now. Since the laws are contained in the Mosaic Covenant, they were highly relevant to the Jews who made up the nation. Those laws were written for those Israelites, and they were obligated to fulfill them in their covenantal relationship with God. Today, when we as God's people read those laws, they can seem distant and irrelevant, because often they are to some degree. Those laws were for people under a different covenant. We as modern believers are related to the same God, so some ideas and even some laws carry into our covenant, but the laws of the Old Testament were originally for Israelites living under the Mosaic Covenant.

Believers today relate to God through faith in Jesus, so we are under the New Covenant. As we already have seen, the New Covenant replaced the Mosaic Covenant, so in one sense, the laws of the Mosaic Covenant do not apply to us. But it is also easy to see that a number of things from the Mosaic Covenant do carry over to the New Covenant.

It could be compared to my working at a company in one position in one department and being transferred to a different position in another department in the same company. Some parts of my old position carried through to my new position without changing (some responsibilities, seniority for years of service, even my salary), whereas other things clearly did change (my boss, my schedule, most of my responsibilities). Likewise, the New Covenant kept some things from the Old Testament (same God, same need for righteousness and holiness), but clearly changed other things (the object of our faith, many of the rules). Thus some of the laws from the Mosaic Covenant continue in the New Covenant as taught in the New Testament (honor God above all, do not murder) but many do not (sacrifice animals to cover sin, travel to Jerusalem to observe certain Jewish holidays). We are now under the New Covenant and relate to God by the guidelines of the New Covenant.

What value, then, do the laws of the Old Testament have for us now and how should we relate to them? If guideline #5 works, then we should see if the laws of the Mosaic Covenant also appear in the New Covenant. If they do, we know that they are still valid today. If the old laws don't reappear, then we can assume that they are no longer valid. But even if they are no longer valid, they still have some value to us. They illustrate how God's people related to him in an earlier day, and we can learn from that. Most often, we can see how the same principle is practiced in a different way under the New Covenant. This helps us see the continuity in God's relationship to his people (like taking care of one another) without tying us down to outdated rules (like building fences around our roofs).

Guidelines

How should we then approach the laws of the Old Testament? We'll discuss this more in the final chapter, but in brief, I usually find it useful to study the context of a law to learn what God was teaching the original audience and how they were to obey it. I then check to see if the same rule or principle—or perhaps an updated version of it—reappears in the New Testament. If the rules are the same, the old rule still applies (Do not commit adultery). If God has updated it, I try to appreciate the old rule, clarify the connection to the new form, and then focus on the new version as what is applicable to us. This helps me appreciate the past while also recognizing changes and allowing me to feel okay about setting aside things that seem irrelevant. Sometimes they are. Again, we'll come back to this in the final chapter and expand on it.

So, what's next? One particular area where God has clearly updated the rules for relating to him is the area of sacrifice. God expected people under the Mosaic Covenant to cover their sins and express to others their relationship to him through various sacrifices. These are explained in great detail in the book of Leviticus. Since Leviticus is a particular challenge to modern believers, let's discuss that book next.

Study Questions

1. Do you enjoy reading through the laws in the Old Testament? Why or why not?

2. After reading this chapter, how would you describe the purpose(s) for the laws in the Old Testament?

3. Which of the following approaches to the relationship between Old Testament laws and the New Testament do you find most helpful and why?
   a. All Old Testament laws still apply to modern Christians unless cancelled by the New Testament.

b. Only the moral laws of the Old Testament still apply; this excludes the religious and civil laws.
c. Only the Ten Commandments still apply.
d. Only the moral principles behind Old Testament laws still apply.
e. The only Old Testament laws that still apply fully are those repeated in the New Testament.

3

Learning to Appreciate Leviticus
(at Least a Little)

The Problem—Why Is the Book of Leviticus So Hard to Appreciate?

This chapter deals with the book of Leviticus, one of the most difficult books in the Bible for modern Christians to appreciate. Because Leviticus contains laws given by God to ancient Israel, the preceding chapter addressed Leviticus in a general way. However, given the extra-challenging nature of Leviticus with its detailed laws about outdated sacrifices and regulations about seemingly obscure issues like mildew, it deserves a chapter all its own.

One student named Elyse described well the challenges with Leviticus when she wrote, "The most boring part of the Bible for me has always been the laws in the Pentateuch, specifically *the book of Leviticus*. Repetition of laws and details of sacrifices makes the text somewhat tedious"—I think she understated that point—"and the overall foreignness of the topics makes the book seem unapproachable."

Leviticus does indeed seem unapproachable to most modern readers of the Bible. It focuses on holiness, which we can appreciate to some degree, but does so mostly by citing rules that appear strange and/or irrelevant. In addition, the book starts out by describing in great detail a number of sacrifices the ancient Israelites carried out in their worship of God—sacrifices that modern Christians understand have been rendered obsolete by the sacrifice of Jesus. Leviticus then continues with rules about the priests under the Israelite religious system, but now all believers are considered priests rather than just one line of people as in the Old Testament. So Leviticus starts by discussing matters that are now largely irrelevant, but does the rest of the book get any better?

After the rules about sacrifices and priests, the rest of Leviticus gives regulations about various other issues, a number of which are unpleasant—mildew, skin diseases, and bodily discharges. Why so gross? Perhaps it's partly because the book doubled as an ancient medical guide of sorts and medicine must deal with some unpleasant issues. Even subjects such as distinguishing between foods that are clean and unclean seem to offer little for the modern reader.

Another student named Isaac addressed this disconnect with his humorous paraphrase of a law found in Leviticus: "If the uncloven hoof of a cloven-hoofed animal is not cloven, you shall cleave it, and it is clean." He continued with an honest evaluation and admission: "You would need to work very hard to find any meaningful passages in Leviticus that apply to modern life. I am not usually willing to work THAT hard." Nor are many others, Isaac. Leviticus can seem awfully distant, mundane, and irrelevant to our world today.

So what can Leviticus offer to the modern reader of the Bible, given that so much of what it says has been eclipsed by teaching in the New Testament? Plenty. Let's start by discussing the original purposes and lessons that the book had for the ancient Israelites, and then move on to see what we can learn from this seemingly distant, uninteresting book of the Bible. If you are at all like me, you may be pleasantly surprised at what we can find hidden in plain sight in Leviticus. The book actually has much to say about God, how we should relate to him, and how we should live—assuming we frame the discussion properly.

The Point—What Purposes Did Leviticus Originally Serve?

The context of Leviticus

Before discussing the purposes Leviticus originally served, let's set the book in its proper historical and religious context. That's helpful for any book in the Bible, but for Leviticus more than most. According to the historical narrative given through the Pentateuch, the book of Leviticus was set in the time shortly after the Israelites had left Egypt. These people had been freed from slavery, escaped from Egypt, witnessed God's defeat of the Egyptian military, and continued their journey into the desert of the Sinai Peninsula to make their great national covenant with God and formalize their relationship with him. They traveled to and camped in front of one of the many granite mountains in the region, which the Bible calls Mount Sinai. They remained camped in front of the mountain for more than a year, during which time they committed themselves to the Mosaic Covenant, built the Tabernacle, and received from God the laws they would need for their society and their religion. Leviticus is part of that revelation.

Thus, the book is part of how God helped the Israelites establish themselves as a nation and set up a system of worship. The rules in Leviticus may seem distant to modern Christian readers of the Bible, but for the Israelites of the time, those rules helped them know how to properly relate to God and to their fellow countrymen. But since modern Christians aren't part of that Israelite nation, and the worship in which we participate has changed dramatically, the book is much less relevant to us. These changes don't lessen the book's original importance, though. Let's learn more about the importance of Leviticus by looking further at its content and purpose.

The content of Leviticus

Though the book had great significance to its original audience and still has much to teach a modern audience, it isn't packaged in a friendly fashion for today's readers. It starts with just one brief verse of introduction before launching into several chapters describing sacrifices in great detail. Although these precise descriptions would have helped both the ancient Israelites know what was required of them and the priests know how to do their part to carry out those sacrifices, the detail doesn't hold the interest of modern readers and may even cloud the importance of the sacrifices.

These detailed descriptions of the sacrifices begin the first of two major sections of the book, both of which tell the Israelites how to conduct themselves properly in their relationship to God. One section emphasizes the rules for their religious system, and the other focuses more on their daily lives. The first section (chapters 1–16) tells the Israelites how to conduct their religious activity by offering proper sacrifices (1–7) made through properly consecrated priests (8–10) and by following the right rules of purification (11–15). The book pivots with the description of the Day of Atonement (16), the annual event when the entire nation would experience cleansing (more on this later). The second section (17–27) focuses more on laws for daily living with rules for various practices—sexual relations, priests, feasts (17–25)—followed by blessings and curses for proper and improper conduct (26), and finally instructions on how to fulfill vows (27), an important part of religious life in the ancient Near East.

The purpose of Leviticus

Both of these sections of Leviticus emphasize how the Israelites could manifest holiness, clearly the main theme of Leviticus. In fact, various forms of the term *holy* appear more than one hundred times in the book. The first of the two main sections tell how the Israelites should manifest holiness as a group, and the second explains how they should demonstrate holiness as individuals. But what exactly is holiness? What does the word mean? Obviously it is important, since it describes God and his expectation for his people (both in the past and in the present).

The term *holy* can mean a number of things, both in the Bible and in the world out of which the Bible came. The biblical concept of holiness is largely similar to that of surrounding cultures, but it also differs meaningfully in at least a few aspects. We will summarize the varying concepts of holiness with two individual but related ideas—*separation* and *purity*.

In one respect, something is holy because it is *separated* from other things. This is true for God and for the things associated with him; God is holy in part because he is distinct and separate from everything else that exists. He is different; he is other; he is distinct from all created things. In the same way, things that are consecrated or separated for divine service are also holy because they have been separated from other similar things. The Israelites were holy because God separated them from the surrounding peoples. "You are to be holy to me because I . . . have set you apart from the nations to be my own" (Leviticus 20:26). Priests in the Old Testament were holy people because they were set apart from other people in order to serve God. The seventh day was holy because it was set apart from the other six days, and so on.

Other cultures around Israel shared the understanding that holiness meant separation. The people in these other cultures also considered their gods different from humans, so their gods were holy. Likewise, anything or anyone that was set apart for divine use or service (offerings, priests) was also holy, as with Israel.

But we also find an important difference between the biblical concept of holiness and that of nearby cultures. The gods of other cultures sometimes did not reflect the upright, moral character of Israel's God, but they were still thought of as holy. Some of these gods lied and committed brutal or immoral acts, yet were still holy because they were gods and separate from humans. Anything or anyone set apart for them was also holy, no matter its quality or character. Thus, when the worship of these other gods included prostitutes who helped the worshipers participate in rites of fertility, even the prostitutes were considered holy!

This apparent mismatch with the biblical idea of holiness arose because these gods or people were set apart, but they didn't share the other major aspect of biblical holiness— *purity.* The God of Israel was separate, but he was also holy because he was completely *pure in character.* He stood apart from humanity both in *kind* and in *character.* He didn't share the character flaws of humanity, and he expected his people to rise above their flaws and reflect his pure character instead. "I am the Lord, who brought you up out of Egypt to be your God; therefore be holy, because I am holy" (Leviticus 11:45).

The Israelites needed this instruction on holiness because of their relationship to their holy God. Leviticus told the Israelites how to be holy as God required. Modern readers may struggle to see the value of Leviticus, but for ancient Israel, it played an essential role in their religious life.

The Goal—What Lessons Did Leviticus Teach the Israelites?

Along with telling the Israelites *what* they should do both in worship and in their daily lives, Leviticus demonstrates *why* they should do it. They needed to exhibit holiness because they were related by covenant to a God who was holy, and he expected them to reflect that holiness as well. Because they weren't reflecting his holiness, God established sacrifices to cover their sin. In addition to offering proper sacrifices, the Israelites needed to reflect holiness in their everyday lives. They did this by following rules about all manner of things, including unpleasant topics such as skin diseases and bodily discharges. Though some of these rules appear strange to us, the ancient Israelites probably understood the need to obey them—following the rules helped them to manifest holiness.

Israel's God was holy

As noted already, holiness constitutes the main theme of Leviticus. God is holy by separation and by purity and requires the same of his people. This proved difficult and led to the next aspect of holiness found in Leviticus.

God expected his people to be holy

The holy God of Israel required that his people share in his holiness. They were to do this by keeping all the decrees and obeying the laws God had given (Leviticus 20:22), which of course they couldn't do all the time. Rather than reflecting holiness, the Israelites often failed to conform to God's laws. The Bible refers to this failure as sin, and makes it clear that sin separates people from God. Leviticus explains that some sin is intentional, while other shortcomings are the result of living in a fallen world. For example, a woman who gave birth didn't sin, but that process made her ritually impure, so she needed to be purified (Leviticus 12). So whether they chose badly or simply had things happen to them, the Israelites inevitably found themselves unholy, separated from God, and in danger of judgment.

God carried out a plan to make his people holy

Since the holy God expected holiness from people who couldn't maintain that holiness, God had to intervene and resolve this problem. He did this through what the Bible calls *atonement*. Atonement is what I like to call a five-dollar religious word, one that we probably hear in church and may use, but not fully know what it means. The central idea of atonement is "covering," in which God covers the sin of his people so he no longer sees it. This covering deflects God's anger against the sin in his people, and thus reconciles them to him. Atonement reconciles an unholy people to a holy God.

How was this atonement or reconciliation accomplished in ancient Israel? Through appropriate sacrifices that covered the sin. "Come to the altar and sacrifice your sin offering and your burnt offering and make atonement for yourself and the people . . . as the Lord has commanded" (Leviticus 9:7). Because sacrifices were so important, this book on holiness begins by describing sacrifices, some of which atoned for the sins of the people. After describing sacrifices, Leviticus then describes priests, the intermediaries responsible for carrying out the sacrifices that reconciled the holy God with his unholy people. Thus the book focuses on the means for God's people to be made right with him.

These sacrifices offered by the people through the priests were effective in part because of the annual Day of Atonement (Leviticus 16). On this holiest of all days the sacrifices that atoned for the sin of the entire nation were made. On the Day of Atonement, the high priest sacrificed an animal, entered the Holy of Holies in the temple, and sprinkled the atoning blood of that sacrifice. He continued by confessing the sins of the nation over a goat, which was then sent off into the deserted wilderness. This act atoned for the sins of the people for another year, reconciling them to God.

Students often ask me how people in the Old Testament were saved, since they sacrificed animals rather than trusting in Jesus, who had not yet died to atone for their sins. The key to comprehending the faith of the Old Testament believers is in understanding that these people participated in the proper acts of atonement that God had prescribed for their time, which would eventually culminate in the death of Jesus. If they made the required sacrifices with the proper attitude, that act of faith covered their sin. Those required sacrifices then culminated in the annual atonement brought about by the proper sacrifices on the Day of Atonement. And those annual acts of faith covered the sins of the nation and pointed to the ultimate atonement brought about by Jesus' sacrifice.

The sacrifices required in Leviticus, and the rest of the Old Testament, were effective but temporary. They accomplished atonement but had to be continuously repeated until Jesus could atone for sin once for all time. His faithful act sealed the atonement accomplished by the countless sacrifices that had preceded him, and made possible forgiveness for the countless sins that would follow him, as long as those subsequent sinners trusted in his atoning death. People in the Old Testament were saved because they acted in faith in the manner God required at that point in history, and their acts would eventually connect to Jesus.

God expected his people to live in a way that reflected God's holiness

Once God reconciled himself to his people, he expected them to live in a way that corresponded to what they had experienced. God had chosen and set his people apart. They couldn't live up to his standard of holiness, so he made possible atonement through sacrifice. As a response, their humble and repentant hearts should desire the things of God rather than the things of the world, including following the rules that

God had laid out for them. This enabled them to participate in God's holiness through what they were and what they did, and it gave honor to God in the eyes of other believers as well as nonbelievers. God expected his people to live holy lives that reflected the character of a holy God.

The Benefit—What Can We Learn Today From Leviticus and Its Emphasis on Holiness?

So what can we modern believers learn from Leviticus, a book of sacrifices and priests and laws about odd things? Despite reflecting a religious system that is now outdated in certain key aspects, Leviticus still has much to teach the modern Christian. It shows that God cares deeply about holiness, that sin is very serious, and that our lives should still reflect God's holiness.

God is very concerned about holiness

As we have already noted, holiness is intrinsic to God's nature and to his character. It is an inseparable part of what he is and what he is like. He longs for his people to share in that holiness, which we do to some degree. We are holy in that God has set us apart for himself, and we are holy because God has made us holy through the atoning sacrifice of Jesus. What God is, and what his Son died for, is what he wants us to live out. Holiness is *very* important to our holy God. It should be equally important to us.

Sin is serious and has always been costly

Even though holiness is the aspiration of the Christian, our fallen nature causes us to make some choices contrary to what our holy God expects and what our new nature desires. Those choices create a barrier between us and God. For those who never trust in Jesus' death to reconcile them to God, their sin will ultimately lead to their judgment. For those who have trusted in Jesus' atoning death, their sinful choices create conflict in them and in their relationship with God and with others.

The problem of sin is serious. The ancient Israelites had to sacrifice perfect animals to satisfy a holy God. Killing valuable animals was costly. Most Israelites had a very limited number of livestock, and those animals represented a significant part of their wealth and an important source of food and other products. Laying them on the altar represented a true sacrifice. God accepted these to atone for sin in antiquity, and later allowed the sacrifice of his own Son to cover the sin of men and women and reconcile them to himself. Sin is and has always been costly.

Modern believers still need to reflect God's holiness

Just as God expected his people in Old Testament times to reflect his character through holy living, so he expects it of us now. Today we have the advantage of a fuller revelation as well as the indwelling Holy Spirit to guide and empower us to live holy lives consistent with God's character, manifesting virtues such as love, joy, peace, and kindness (Galatians 5:22–23) and obeying God's commands in the New Testament. Though we will inevitably fail at times, we have less excuse than God's people did during the time of the Old Testament.

What God required of Israelites under the Mosaic Covenant, he requires of modern believers under the New Covenant. Our God is a holy God. His people should reflect that holiness.

Conclusion

The main themes of Leviticus have not been made obsolete, even though the means to accomplish them and the manner of expressing them have changed. We follow our God through faith in Jesus Christ. Our guidelines for holy living are not based on outdated rules about mildew and skin diseases; the guidelines in the New Testament often teach a higher way. For example, in Matthew 5:27–28, we are reminded of the command not to commit adultery and are told that one who lusts after a woman has already committed adultery with her in his heart. I find a rule about what I think and desire more relevant—and challenging—than a rule simply about what I do. It's also eminently appropriate if I aim to truly reflect God's holiness in my era.

Leviticus has hidden a number of good things in not-so-plain sight. It has much to teach modern Christians, but as seen at the beginning of this chapter, we need to remember to frame the explanation appropriately. In Leviticus, the holy God gave rules to the ancient Israelites so they could fulfill the requirement to be holy. Likewise, he expects holiness of modern believers, and gives us similar but updated guidelines in the New Testament.

Next, we will move to another difficult, but different, part of the Bible. Joshua, chapters 13–21, describes the land divisions the various tribes of Israel were to inherit after the conquest. This part of the Bible is both similar to and different from the laws and rules that we have discussed in the last two chapters. Joshua doesn't contain outdated laws so much as it details a matter that is unfamiliar, obscure, and at first glance irrelevant to the modern reader. But we may find some gems hidden in plain sight there as well.

Study Questions

1. Do you enjoy reading through the book of Leviticus? Why or why not?

2. To whom was Leviticus originally written? For what purpose?

3. How did Leviticus teach the ancient Israelites to deal with their sin? Can this teach us anything about dealing with our sin?

4. What does Leviticus teach us about God's holiness and our need for holiness?

4

What Should We Do With the Land Divisions in Joshua 13–21?

The Problem—Why Is the Second Half of Joshua So Irrelevant?

People reading through the Bible typically have a rather mixed experience going through the book of Joshua. The first half of the book is interesting and enjoyable; the second half not so much. In the first half of Joshua, we read the exciting story of the Israelites conquering their long-promised land, faithfully obeying (usually) God's commands so they can secure a homeland for themselves and their descendants. The accounts of the spying, the battles, and unusual military strategy fire the imagination and challenge a reader's courage and faith. The second half of Joshua, by contrast, quickly bogs down with detailed descriptions of land divisions and designations, including long lists of place names that are unfamiliar.

So what should we do with Joshua 13–21? And why is this section included in the Bible in the first place? Sometimes I wonder if it wasn't inconsiderate of the early writer(s) to include such irrelevant information. Let's see if we can't find something valuable in these chapters by looking at the original purpose(s) for this section and what the original audience should have learned from it. Hopefully that will help us see which ideas, if any, flow into the New Testament and apply to our world, telling us more about what God has done for us as believers and how we should respond.

The Point—What Purposes Did Joshua 13–21 Originally Serve?

Joshua 13–21 served several purposes for the original audience of the book. First, it functioned as a type of hinge in the story contained in Joshua, just as the book functioned as a hinge in the greater story of the nation. Joshua 13–21 documented vital information about the land the tribes were to inherit. It also demonstrated God's faithfulness to fulfill his promise to give Israel a homeland, a fulfillment for which the Israelites waited literally centuries. Let's discuss each of these purposes in depth.

A *hinge within a hinge*

As we have said, this section serves as a hinge within the book of Joshua, and the whole book serves as a hinge in the flow of the entire Old Testament. The book of Joshua connects the Pentateuch (Genesis through Deuteronomy) to the rest of the Old Testament by forming a fitting conclusion to the earliest parts of the Bible and setting the stage for the rest of the Old Testament. The people of Israel (beginning with Abraham and the other patriarchs) eventually found themselves enslaved in Egypt, yearning for a land of their own where they could establish themselves as a nation. The books of Exodus through Deuteronomy recount the next events as Moses led Israel toward nationhood—theologically, socially, and geographically.

The book of Joshua concludes this process as the Israelites established themselves in the land where the rest of the events of the Old Testament would play out. Joshua shows the placing of the Israelites in the location where they would be able to demonstrate their faithfulness to God and rise to regional dominance. The land would also witness their covenantal infidelity, for which God would eventually expel them from the land, but afterward restore them to it. The book of Joshua concludes the first major period in Israelite history and introduces the second.

In chapters 1–12, the Israelites enter Canaan and conquer its hilly heartland. Chapters 13–21 lay out the land allotments for the different tribes, with a few related stories and comments. The final chapters (22–24) tell us the beginning of what happened to the Israelites in Canaan. We read about their settling into the land, their lack of a leader to follow Joshua, and tensions between the tribes, helping to set the stage for the turbulent period of Judges–Kings that would follow.

Land designations and borders in detail

Along with serving as a hinge in the account of Israel's conquest and national history, Joshua 13–21 also records in great detail the sections of land inherited by the twelve tribes of Israel and what the boundaries were. Detailed land descriptions don't make for interesting reading, but they can make for more peaceful lives. We don't appreciate these details in part because we don't need the information. It's of little interest to us where the border lines were drawn between tribes, but if we had been members of these tribes the details would have proven valuable. For the original audience of the book, this section of Joshua told them where their tribal homes and farmlands would be located, and would have

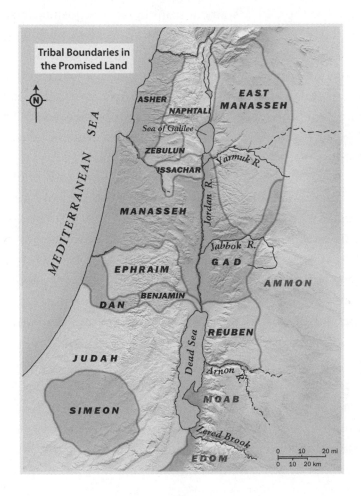

helped avoid disputes over land ownership down through the centuries.

The importance of clear land descriptions in avoiding conflict became abundantly clear to my family during the final years that we lived in Israel. We rented the brand-new home of a couple who had built it but then chose to rent it out for a few years before moving in. We enjoyed their new home, but we also experienced some of their conflict as well. Our owners were the first to build on a strip of land being developed in a small village. They bought one of the lots, had a surveyor plot out the lot lines, then laid out the location of their house and built accordingly. One side of the house supposedly stood one meter from the lot line, according to the minimum distance required by the local zoning laws. Unfortunately, the surveyor hadn't laid out the lot lines correctly.

We lived in the house for perhaps two years before anyone discovered the problem. By that time another family had purchased the lot next to ours and prepared to build their home. Their preparations brought to light the fact that our home infringed on the mutual property line. The house wasn't only too close to the line; it actually crossed it and stood on a part of the neighbors' lot. *Big problem.* Our family avoided much of the issue, as it fell to our landlords and the original surveyor to sort out the mess with the neighbors. The conflict lasted for years, and when I last spoke to our former landlord, some sixteen years after we had left Israel, he and the neighbors were still feuding over the issue. Clear boundaries can be critical to avoiding problems like this one. That experience gave me more patience and understanding when reading the detailed land descriptions such as we find in the book of Joshua.

God was faithful and fulfilled his promises

The Israelites needed to know clearly where the land boundaries lay and they also needed to know clearly that they were in covenant with a God who faithfully fulfilled his promises. As mentioned earlier in this chapter, God had promised that he would give the land of Canaan to the nation of Israel. Though it took a *very long* time, God came through at the time of Joshua and gave Israel their long-anticipated land.

God first promised Canaan to Israel during the time of Abraham: "The Lord appeared to Abram [as he was originally called] and said, 'To your offspring I will give this land' " (Genesis 12:7). God would repeat that promise to Abraham and in the following years to his descendants, but it would take many generations before he fulfilled it. Although the dating of Abraham's life and the conquest under Joshua are debated, the time that elapsed between the promise and the fulfillment may have been as much as 800 years! Even if it had been only 400 years, the Israelites as a nation had waited incredibly long, but God had been incredibly faithful to fulfill his promise. The Israelites needed to understand and *remember* God's faithfulness, because they would need to demonstrate faithfulness in return.

On a side note, when the Bible uses the term *remember* it usually means to keep something in mind in order to act correctly. Today, *remember* typically means "to recall some fact." The Israelites weren't supposed to merely *think about* God's faithfulness, they were to think about it and *act properly in light of it.* This is why we find the command to "remember" so often in Deuteronomy. Moses was challenging the Israelites to *keep in mind* all God had done for them as a nation in getting them to the edge of Canaan and then *act accordingly* by remaining faithful to their covenant with God once they had conquered Canaan.

The Goal—What Lessons Did Joshua 13–21 Teach the Israelites?

Just as Joshua chapters 13–21 demonstrated God's faithfulness to Israel, so it encouraged the Israelites to demonstrate their faithfulness to God. In addition, this section of the book of Joshua would have encouraged them to continue and complete their conquest of the land. It also should have helped them learn that keeping that land in the coming generations would depend on their continued fidelity to their national covenant with God.

Israel needed to remain faithful to God

God had been faithful, and Israel had cashed in. What he had promised to Abraham centuries earlier, God had fulfilled by giving this generation the land of Canaan. Israel had benefitted from God's faithfulness. Would they exhibit the same faithfulness to God?

Israel had a rather checkered history when it came to faithfulness. Even the patriarchs had a blemished record. In each generation, the patriarchal ancestors had demonstrated remarkable faithfulness as well as great failure. Then after the Exodus from Egypt, their great leader Moses led the Israelites well in the most trying of circumstances but had also failed dramatically. The nation as a whole had survived their time in the wilderness, but they had also failed so badly that a whole generation had been lost. The subsequent generation had conquered Canaan, but what would they do after that?

God laid out the challenge clearly: "Be very strong; be careful to obey all that is written in the Book of the Law of Moses, without turning aside to the right or to the left. . . . You are to hold fast to the Lord your God, as you have until now" (Joshua 23:6, 8). Such was their great challenge, and it would play out both in the near term and in the distant future, both in how they handled the rest of the conquest and how well they would be able to hold on to their land in the years to come.

Israel needed to complete the conquest

The first way in which Israel would demonstrate its faithfulness was in how they would complete the conquest of Canaan. They had already defeated many of the armies of the Canaanites, but they had not dispossessed the Canaanites entirely. Defeating an army isn't necessarily the same as taking over the land that the army protects. Israel had accomplished much, but there was much more to do.

This difference in what was done and what was left to do connects to one of the problems that many careful readers have with the book of Joshua. On the one hand, the book states clearly that Israel had decisively defeated the Canaanites: "So Joshua took this entire land. . . . He captured all their kings and put them to death. . . . So Joshua took the entire land, just as the Lord had directed Moses, and he gave it as an inheritance to Israel according to their tribal divisions" (Joshua 11:16–17, 23). This is the language of fulfilled promises, stating that God had helped Israel just as he had promised.

But the book also states that much land remained unconquered. This may seem contradictory to the modern reader, but apparently it wasn't to the ancient audience. The author was saying that God fulfilled his promise to give Israel the land, and much work still remained. Both were true. "When Joshua had grown old, the Lord said to him, 'You are very old, and there are still very large areas of land to be taken over. This is the land that remains. . . .'" (Joshua 13:1–2). Although God had fulfilled his promises, he left more work for Israel to complete. They needed to continue the process of conquest by driving out the rest of the people and taking over the rest of the land. Just as they couldn't accomplish the first part without God's help, neither could they do the remainder on their own. But to receive God's continued help, the Israelites needed to demonstrate continued loyalty to their covenant with God, and the question remained—would they?

Israel needed to understand that keeping their land depended on their covenantal loyalty

Additionally, Israel needed to bear in mind that keeping the land depended on their fidelity to their covenant with God. God had made an *unconditional* promise to Abraham that he would *give the land* to Israel and had fulfilled that promise by the end of the book of Joshua. Now God promised that Israel could *keep that land* and enjoy it—but this promise was *conditional*. The great national covenant that God made with Israel, which we often call the Mosaic Covenant, was a conditional covenant. In it, God promised Israel many blessings, including fertility and keeping the land, but these blessings were based on the condition that Israel remained faithful.

As we know from the rest of the Old Testament, the Israelites managed to hold on to their land for a rather long time, but ultimately lost it because of their infidelity. During the time of the Judges (immediately following Joshua), Israel repeatedly turned from their God. In response, God turned them over to others, but rescued them each time when they repented. In the book of Samuel, the promised King David brought Israel to a place of rest and greatness beyond what Joshua had provided, but it was only temporary. Israel receded from her peaks of size and power. Then in the book of Kings, the repeated disloyalty of Israel and Judah ran God's patience to its limit, so he eventually expelled them from their land, but afterward partially restored them.

The faithful God who had given a homeland to Israel at the time of Joshua demanded faithfulness in return, and Israel's continued hold on the land depended on that faithfulness. Although the Israelites probably understand that at the end of Joshua's career, they and their descendants didn't remain faithful to the covenant they had made with God (Joshua 24). Because of this, they eventually lost their beloved homeland.

The Benefit—What Can We Learn From Joshua 13–21?

We have seen that the rather mundane description of tribal allotments and border descriptions in Joshua 13–21 served a number of good purposes for the early Israelites. It gave clear descriptions of their allotted land, it showed that God had faithfully fulfilled his promises, and it served as a challenge for the Israelites to maintain covenantal loyalty. What can we learn today from this section of Scripture, beyond appreciating its value for its original audience?

God sometimes is slow to carry out his purposes, so we must be patient

Although God is faithful and surely fulfills his promises, we have seen that he can be quite slow (by our estimation) in doing so. The Israelite nation waited centuries for God to give them the land of Canaan. Obviously no individual can wait that long; they had to wait as a continuing people. So too, we as modern believers are waiting for God to fulfill certain promises to us. Before he left the earth following his resurrection, Jesus promised to return. Two thousand years have passed, and still the church waits. But just as surely as God gave Canaan to Israel after his people had waited for centuries, so Jesus will surely return after the church has waited for millennia. We don't know when, but we as an ongoing church continue to anticipate his return.

On a more personal level, I see that God doesn't always make life work out the way that I want, and I must wait to see how he will make things turn out for the best. I think I know what is best, but God seems to have other ideas at times. For example, my wife and I prayed that God would give us healthy children and help us to raise them to walk with him. To our surprise, our fourth child was born mentally and physically handicapped. Though that wasn't what we wanted or expected, we know that God has promised to make all situations work for the good of those who love him (Romans 8:28). Though we don't fully understand God's purposes for our sweet, beloved daughter, we continue to trust God and wait for him to work out his will for us and for her.

God doesn't promise us land, but a better relationship and a better fellowship

God promised Canaan to the Israelites and gave them that land. The Israelites had committed themselves to God under the Mosaic Covenant and kept the land as long as they were faithful. We as modern believers relate to God under a New Covenant, and it contains some of the same promises as the Mosaic Covenant. The same God calls modern believers to covenantal loyalty, but under a different covenant, and some of the promises have changed.

God has promised us a different inheritance with different covenantal partners. We are not promised part of the land of Canaan. Though we are promised the earth in some fashion (Matthew 5:5), our ultimate inheritance is kept in heaven (1 Peter 1:3–5). And it is not only Israelites who form the membership of the new covenantal community. God has included Gentiles as well (Isaiah 56:3–7; 66:18–23). In addition to what we are promised and who can become members of God's kingdom, the kingdom has dramatically changed as well. We don't live in a geographically bound entity led by God's chosen human ruler, we live as citizens of a nonphysical, spiritual kingdom (Colossians 1:13–14).

We can enjoy a better rest than the Israelites, and anticipate our final rest

As the Israelites at the time of Moses marched toward Canaan at the close of their time in the wilderness, they must have longed for a place to settle down and call home. This is what the Bible calls "rest" (Joshua 1:13). The Israelites won that rest to a degree under Joshua, and to a greater degree later under David. By the close of the book of Joshua, they had begun to enjoy their promised rest, but the fullness of that would come later for them as a nation. Unfortunately, they ultimately would lose their land altogether (though God would later restore it to them).

Likewise, we as believers today have begun to enjoy our promised eternal life, but will experience it more fully later. We have been granted a greater, though different, rest than what the Israelites enjoyed in Israel, through our faith in Jesus (Hebrews 4:1–11). For now we enjoy the loving fellowship of a new community of believers, and ultimately we will enjoy the final fulfillment of that rest when we dwell with God face-to-face in the New Jerusalem (Revelation 21–22). Our hope is less tangible than the promise of living in Israel, but when it is fulfilled it will last for eternity.

Conclusion

Joshua 13–21 forms a hinge in the story of Israel taking possession of Canaan. The Israelites had fought the battles that gained the land God had promised. Now they were settling in to enjoy what God had promised and needed clear border descriptions to avoid problems, to remind them that God had been faithful, and to challenge them to respond with similar faithfulness.

Next, let's discuss a type of biblical material most people find truly boring—the genealogies. These lists can be tedious— at least for the modern reader. But though they are often dreary for us, it's not too difficult to figure out why they were important for the first readers of the Bible. And with a little digging we can find some rather interesting things that God has hidden in plain sight—even in the genealogies. Perhaps you're thinking, *Really? Interesting stuff in the genealogies?* Really. Come on, I'll show you.

Study Questions

1. Do you enjoy reading the book of Joshua? How would you compare chapters 13–21 with chapters 1–12?

2. What purposes did Joshua 13–21 serve the Israelites who first settled Canaan?

3. How does Joshua 13–21 reflect God's faithfulness to fulfill his promises?

4. The ancient Israelites found their rest by living in the land God had promised them. According to Hebrews 4:1–11, what rest should modern Christians enjoy? According to Revelation 21–22, what will be our final rest?

5

Learning From Dull Genealogies

The Problem: Why Are Genealogies Boring?

If you're like most readers of the Bible, you're less than thrilled when you come to one of the many genealogies scattered throughout Scripture. On the other hand, a lot of modern readers, including me, *are* interested in our own genealogies and family stories. I find it fascinating to trace my family back as many generations as possible to learn when and where my ancestors lived, how they came to America, and what they went through in their part of the chain of humanity that eventually linked to me. I find *those* genealogies very interesting because I'm connected to them.

I have also discovered that historical realities connected to my family lines often take on new meaning. For example, I had long known a little about the Battle of Waterloo, in which the French emperor Napoleon suffered his final defeat, but I wasn't particularly interested in it. That all changed when

I learned that one of my German ancestors fought in the Prussian army that helped defeat Napoleon and his French forces at Waterloo. All of a sudden I wanted to learn everything I could about the battle. Who was involved? How did the events play out? Did Napoleon make some great mistake that led to his loss? And most important, what role did the Prussians (and thus, my ancestor) play in the battle? Since I was now connected to the event, it took on a whole new level of significance for me.

So why do I find my own family genealogies and histories interesting, but not the genealogies in the Bible? Perhaps it's because I lack a personal connection to them. The people in the Bible might be my spiritual ancestors, but I don't feel as closely connected to them as I do to those whose blood runs in my veins. I think this disconnect is why biblical genealogies come across to the modern reader as boring and irrelevant. They don't connect to *our* story.

When we consider the challenge of reading biblical genealogies, it is helpful to remember that those stories and their connected genealogies weren't originally written for modern readers. Certainly God's Word has application to people like us in later ages, but the biblical material, including the genealogies, was first written primarily to Jews in ancient Israel, and they were connected by blood as well as spiritual heritage to the people listed there. The genealogies helped tell their stories and give their family histories. That must have made the material much more relevant and interesting to them. Remembering this helps me better appreciate the genealogies for what they are—a part of someone else's story.

Even if we acknowledge that biblical genealogies weren't originally written for us, can we still appreciate and learn from them? Do these seemingly pointless lists tell us anything that will help us grow spiritually? Indeed they do. So let's take a look at some additional purposes for these ancient records. We will want to explore why God included them in his holy Word, a book that was destined to be read by a much broader audience than the original readers. We will also look at some of the interesting points of meaning and application that the authors wove into the genealogies. As we take this journey, I'm going to use the genealogy in Genesis 5 as our primary example. Can this ancient list of people connecting Adam to Noah possibly have anything hidden in plain sight? Let's dig in and find out!

The Point: Why Did the Israelites Use Genealogies?

Most of the purposes for biblical genealogies grew out of that society's organization around families and clans. While our culture thinks more in terms of the individual, they thought in terms of the group. Who was a person's father? From what clan did they come? To what tribe did they belong? Then, based on a person's connections, one would know what ancestral rights and obligations applied to them.

Determining One's Occupation and Rights

An ancient Israelite's occupation might well be determined by his family line. If a man descended from Moses' brother Aaron, he was a priest. There was no choice or negotiation involved. A man could not decide to study to become a priest or get himself elected or designated as one. That right and obligation came through his bloodline. The same was true of royalty. If a boy's father was the king, he would be a prince

83

and perhaps the next king. These important jobs were purely an issue of family lineage, so tracking a person's bloodline was paramount.

However, only a relatively small number of Israelites were priests or royalty; most were farmers. But much of a farmer's life revolved around his family connections too. Each person belonged to an extended family called a "father's house," apparently made up of the oldest living male family member plus all those descended from him. Grandparents, parents, aunts and uncles, siblings and cousins all formed their nuclear family. They probably all lived in the same home as well, in a complex of connected rooms, typically organized around a central courtyard.

Then a number of these extended families made up a larger grouping we'll call a "clan." Members of a clan lived near one another and carried out various functions together, like mustering for war. Beyond that level of connection, related clans comprised a tribe, which had clearly distinct regions in the land of Israel allotted to them. These allotments dictated where the tribal members lived and what land they could claim. If a person belonged to the tribe of Ephraim, for example, his family had claim to land within the area designated to Ephraim, but not in that of Benjamin, Judah, or any other tribe. Thus, a person's identity developed from their family, clan, and tribe, in increasingly larger circles of related connectedness. Therefore, a person had to know his or her genealogy, even if only orally, and from that record of connections, they found their place in society.

(Re)Establishing Society's Foundations

The need to know such lines of descent explains why the book of 1 Chronicles, for example, starts out with such a large section of genealogy—nine long chapters of it. By the time Chronicles was written, the nation had been conquered and exiled, and now the survivors had returned home to rebuild their society. Records had undoubtedly been forgotten, lost, or destroyed. How could they rebuild society if they didn't know who belonged to whom and where they each had lived? They had to reestablish this foundation before they could function properly, so the chronicler began with a long series of genealogies.

The Goal: What Did Genealogies Add to the Stories Being Told?

Connecting Major Figures in a Narrative

In addition to these societal functions, one can also see literary functions that genealogies perform in a text. Within a longer story or narrative, genealogies serve useful purposes. Genesis, for example, traces the descent and development of mankind from Adam all the way to the generation of Joseph and his eleven brothers. As the story progresses, the author does not dwell on each generation. Rather, he focuses our attention on certain people, and he uses genealogical sections to connect the people of greater importance to one another. He couldn't just skip over large blocks of people altogether, since the sequence of the lesser-known peoples verifies that the major people indeed were connected. The author thus uses genealogical sections to link the major people relatively quickly as well as to indicate the passage of time and develop certain themes.

We see this in the genealogy of Genesis chapter 5. Genesis 1–4 tells about Adam and Eve and their sons, plus more about the family line of Cain, which was not the line that would carry on God's program. Chapter 5 then reverts to Adam, the first main character, and uses genealogy to link to the second major character, Noah, following the family line that would fulfill God's purposes. Chapter 5 moves quickly through ten generations to connect these two major characters. The author couldn't just jump to Noah; he had to show the links in the chain with a very brief treatment of each generation.

Highlighting Certain People

Many find this genealogy in Genesis 5 to be highly repetitive, which it is, but the author does draw attention to certain people and includes some interesting nuggets of information and theological truth. One of the ways he does this is by deviating from his usual pattern in three of the genealogy's ten generations. Let's discuss these highlights and then examine the truths we can learn.

Certain people in a narrative are often emphasized through their position in the genealogy. In the family lines of both Cain and Seth in Genesis 4 and 5, the seventh person is significant. Seven was typically an important number in the ancient Near East, as was the number ten. Often the numbers seven and ten stood for fullness or completeness, and in these genealogies they seem to denote important individuals, possibly to characterize the lines they were in. The seventh generation in the line that descended from Adam through Cain, the non-chosen line, brings the reader to a man named Lamech. Because of the amount of text devoted to him and his wickedness, Lamech stands out (see Genesis 4:19–24).

Similarly, the seventh person from Adam through the line of Seth, the chosen line, is Enoch (5:21–24). Enoch, like Lamech, also stands out, but because of Enoch's godliness rather than his wickedness. The author writes that Enoch "walked [lived in harmony] with God," and at the end of his life he didn't die; instead God simply "took him" (author's translation).

Thus the author of Genesis focuses on the evil Lamech and the godly Enoch, not only by their contrasting characters, but by their being the seventh person in their respective genealogies. He uses these two people as representatives of their lines, emphasizing the difference between those who walked in sin and those who walked by faith.

The Benefit: What Can We Learn and Apply From Genealogies?

So other than to better understand Israelite culture, is there any reason why we should spend valuable study time on genealogies? Do they have any particular devotional value for us? I would say most or all of them do. Let's use the ten-generation genealogy in Genesis 5 to illustrate.

As noted above, Genesis 5 connects the first two major characters in the book, Adam and Noah, just as the book's other major genealogy (Genesis 11:10–26) connects Noah to the third major character, Abraham. Genesis 5 does this with ten generations, a round number that leaves open the possibility that it is actually selective rather than exhaustive. Round numbers in other genealogies support this idea. For example, Matthew gives exactly fourteen (2 x 7) generations in each period, linking Abraham to David, David to the exile, and the exile to Christ (Matthew 1:17).

The author of Genesis goes through the ten generations from Noah to Abraham with a clear, repeating pattern easily recognizable to the reader. "When X had lived *n* years, he fathered Y. X lived another *m* years, and had other sons and daughters. Altogether X lived (*n* + *m*) years, and then he died." The repetition stresses the inevitability of death, which God had promised back in 2:17. That promise was indeed coming true. They were (almost) all dying. But the repetition quickly gets monotonous, threatening to lull the reader to sleep.

Before you doze off, notice that the author breaks the pattern in three of the ten generations. When he does, he seems to present the reader with three little bits of extra theological richness. The first variation comes in the first generation, before settling into the pattern. In 5:1, the author notes that God made the first humans in his likeness. Then, when the genealogy starts in 5:3, Adam didn't only father a son, he had a son "in his likeness, after his image." This clearly continues the idea of the ongoing image, echoing the original creation of pristine humans in Genesis 1:27.

God made Adam in his image, and now Adam had a son in his image. Even though humans had fallen since the original creation, we continue passing on God's image. The fall corrupted humanity, but it did not obliterate our ability to pass on the power to reflect God in some form. We still have spiritual capacity and the right and responsibility to represent God in creation. I find that truth very encouraging. I also find that encouragement tempered by the statement two verses later: Adam died (5:5). Sin did not obliterate the image of God in us or the ability to pass it on, but it did have a permanent and destructive impact.

The second variation in the genealogy's pattern touches on this apparent inevitability of death. Adam could not avoid death, nor could most of the others on the list. But Enoch, the seventh in the line, did, as noted earlier. Enoch didn't simply "live," but rather "walked with God" by living in harmony with him for three hundred years. In the end he didn't even die but "was no more, because God took him" (5:24). Enoch avoided this ultimate symbol of sin's curse, offering hope to humanity that sin will not have the last word. The New Testament then fleshes out this hope more clearly, showing us that believers will live again after death in an eternal perfect state. We broke the rules and broke ourselves a long time ago, but God will ultimately triumph and return us to what life was like before the fall. I find that truth very encouraging as well.

The third and final variation in the genealogy comes with Noah in generation ten. The introduction to Noah includes his father's prophecy (5:29) that Noah would provide relief from the curse given at the fall. Noah thus joins Enoch in offering hope of humanity overcoming the effects of the curse. Not many will overcome death like Enoch, but God does provide some form of rest and relief for those who are righteous.

Such are the points of hope in the seemingly mundane genealogy in Genesis 5. The author connects Adam to Noah and shows that death rules—most of the time. Life is challenging, but we do carry on God's image. We have the hope of ultimately overcoming death, and until then, God promises moments of rest from the struggles of life.

Now let's turn to address an issue in a major historical section of the Bible—the overlap of the books of Kings and Chronicles. Reading these books seems like the Bible did a rewind but didn't get it exactly right. The books cover the same information, but do so differently. Why the repetition and why the differences? Let's explore that issue and find out.

Study Questions

1. What do you make of the genealogies in the Bible? Interesting? Pointless? Something else?

2. Based on the information given in this chapter, what purposes did genealogies serve the ancient Israelites?

3. Do you see how the authors of the Bible could use genealogies to teach certain truths? Could that make genealogies seem more interesting and helpful?

6

Kings and Chronicles— Didn't I Just Read This Stuff?

The Problem—Why Do 1 & 2 Chronicles Repeat 1 & 2 Kings?

The Old Testament contains a great deal of historical information about the nation of Israel, including the books of (1 & 2) Kings and Chronicles. Much of Israel's history is quite interesting, as it traces the entire cycle of life for the nation over approximately 1,500 years. The process included the origin of the Israelite people with Abraham, the nation's birth under Moses and Joshua, the rise to greatness through David, the division and fall under the later kings of Israel and Judah, and finally the exile, return, and rebirth. The reader not only follows this whole process but also benefits from God's perspective as it is woven into these inspired histories.

Although the overall framework portrays this remarkable story, not all of the parts hold the attention of the typical reader. The books of Genesis and Exodus are mostly appealing, but then Leviticus slows the storyline with its taxing descriptions of sacrifices and rules. Next, Numbers preserves an important but sad part of Israel's history with the death of an entire generation because of unfaithfulness, but the book also bogs down in minutiae that seem to lack clear organization. After Numbers, the storyline picks up again and carries on fairly well through the preparation for and conquest of Canaan and the struggles during the Judges and the reign of King Saul, and reaches a peak with the greatness and failures of David and Solomon.

Then the reader comes to the books of 1 & 2 Kings (originally just one book, as is the case with Samuel and Chronicles) that cover the rest of Israel's complex history up to the exile. Kings tells how Israel divided into two nations, experienced periods of strength and weakness, and took part in complex economic, political, and religious interactions with neighboring nations. The books of Kings cover nearly four hundred years and include prophets speaking for God, explaining why Israel's history unfolded as it did and ended so badly for its people.

While the modern reader can usually follow much of the storyline in Kings and appreciate most of what it communicates, what follows gets confusing. Immediately after 1 and 2 Kings, the books of 1 and 2 Chronicles seem to do a rewind and tell the same story—kind of. Chronicles retells the same period of Israelite history, which is troubling by itself. Why repeat what the previous books just said? As my student Anna Rose said, "I find the books of 1 and 2 Chronicles hard to read because they feel so repetitive after 1 and 2 Kings."

But there's more to the Kings-Chronicles problem. Chronicles also changes the story in some challenging ways. First of all, it begins with a section of nine sleep-inducing chapters of genealogies, which have been aptly called the "Scriptural Sominex." In addition, Chronicles also varies from Kings in some meaningful ways. Whereas Kings included both the good and bad actions of the kings, including the great David and Solomon, Chronicles seems to ignore the bad altogether. And while Kings covered the histories of both Israel and Judah after they split, Chronicles clearly focuses on Judah almost to the exclusion of neighboring Israel.

What gives? Why do these similar books handle this historical information so differently? It's not as if Chronicles can fool the reader (who probably just read Kings) into forgetting the grievous sins of David and Solomon, or that Judah had a sister nation to the north. Why the differences and repetition? If Kings and Chronicles tell basically the same history, do we really need to hear it twice?

The Point—What Purposes Did Kings and Chronicles Originally Serve?

Although Kings and Chronicles look like a similar pair of books covering the same basic information, they actually were written at different times for somewhat different audiences, serving rather different purposes. Let's look at the context for each book to see how and why they differ while still repeating the same basic history.

The Purposes of Kings

The books of Kings continue the basic story of Israelite history that began in Genesis. In fact, they form a somewhat natural ending to the historical flow that runs in a rather straight line through most of the books up to this point in the Bible. In Genesis through Samuel, God created the world, started the people of Israel, gave them a land, and raised them to greatness under David. The books of Kings then cover the next four hundred years from the reign of Solomon through the exile of both Israel and Judah. The books not only record the history, they also explain why the nations fell from prominence and were exiled.

This long history in Kings covers scores of kings and gives a theological evaluation for each, grading each one based on his fidelity to the Mosaic Covenant. Did the king follow the laws of God as David had done? In addition, the king's practice of worship carried special significance for the assessment in Kings. Since God had said to use only one particular place of worship (Deuteronomy 12:4–7), which became Jerusalem when Solomon built the temple there, Kings evaluates whether each king practiced and promoted worship only at the temple in Jerusalem. If he followed God's laws and promoted worship only in Jerusalem, then "he did what was right in the eyes of the Lord." But if the king practiced worship anywhere besides Jerusalem or allowed his people to worship God elsewhere, such as at high places (altars on various hills), then the king "did evil in the eyes of the Lord." The Israelites sometimes worshiped Yahweh at some of these high places (1 Samuel 9:11–27), but after Solomon built the temple, even these were illegitimate, as, of course, were the high places intended for worship of other gods (1 Kings 11:7).

The books of Kings record history using a strong prophetic perspective, telling *about* many of God's prophets or spokesmen, and perhaps written *by* one of those spokesmen. Although Kings does not state who wrote it, a Jewish tradition ascribes its authorship to the prophet Jeremiah. Indeed someone like Jeremiah could have been the author, since the books were clearly written by someone who shared Jeremiah's theological concerns, and its events run basically up to the end of Judah when Jeremiah lived. Even if Jeremiah didn't write Kings, the books are strongly prophetic. They include major stories about a number of prophets, including Nathan, Elijah, and Elisha. They also show repeatedly that what Moses said about true prophets (Deuteronomy 18:21–22) was correct—the predictions of true prophets came true (1 Kings 13:1–32).

The prophetically oriented history in Kings doesn't only record *what* happened, it tells *why it happened*. The books of Kings make it clear that the people of Israel and Judah had not been faithful to the great national covenant (the Mosaic Covenant) they had made with God during their time in the wilderness. God promised them blessings if they would be faithful (Deuteronomy 28:1–14), but warned them of curses such as conquest and exile (Deuteronomy 28:15–68) if they were not. Kings documents how the Israelites failed to live up to their covenantal obligations and were especially guilty of idolatry. As a result, God brought on them the curses that he had promised.

Kings appears to have been written for the Israelites shortly after the nation of Judah had been conquered and sent into exile in Babylon in the early sixth century BC. Nearly a century and a half earlier, the nation of Assyria had conquered the northern nation of Israel and exiled many of its citizens. The southern kingdom of Judah barely survived the Assyrian attacks, and continued as an independent nation for almost another 150 years. Eventually God grew weary of Judah's infidelity and used as his instrument of judgment the nation of Babylon, which by then had risen to dominate that part of the world. Babylon destroyed Jerusalem and Israel's temple and killed or exiled the majority of Judah's population.

The Judeans who survived those horrific events were understandably devastated. Many, if not all, would have lost family members, property, and perhaps their freedom. They had seen their lives irreversibly changed for the worse in nearly every important facet. They had to contend with economic, social, political, and theological wounds. And they must have had questions. How could God have allowed such terrible things to happen to his nation? Weren't the ancient promises to Abraham and David still valid? Why didn't God protect Judah from these heathens? Wasn't Israel's God stronger than the Babylonian gods? If they had sinned, they deserved discipline, but did it need to be so bad? Again, why had all of this happened?

The books of Kings addressed such questions for its audience. They recounted the nation's history, including its sins. They reminded the readers (or hearers) that God had often warned them through the prophets that they had wandered from their covenant and needed to get back on track. He had given them decades, even centuries, to wise up and repent. And when they still did not after all that time and all those warnings, God did what he had promised to do back at the time of Moses (Deuteronomy 28): He enacted the curses of the covenant and brought in foreigners to conquer and exile his people. God was faithful and had fulfilled this harsh part of his covenant with the Israelites.

On the flip side of the same coin, God's faithfulness also gave the Israelites hope for the future. As surely as God had punished his disloyal people according to his promise, so he would be faithful to restore them after decades of punishment as he had also promised. The books of Kings focused on Israel's errors and resulting punishment, but suggested that all was not lost. At the end of 2 Kings, Judah's king, Jehoiachin, was released after thirty-seven years of exile. The Babylonians freed this descendant of David, suggesting that God still had a purpose for the line of David and for the people they had ruled for so long. God's people would not be wiped out completely. They would endure, and God continued to watch out for them. The books of Kings showed clearly that they deserved the punishment that came, but God would also act to give them a future. Such was the message that the audience of Kings needed to hear.

The Purposes of Chronicles

As noted earlier, the books of Chronicles review the same basic Israelite history as had Kings, but for a somewhat different audience and purpose. Chronicles was also written to the Israelites after the exile, but perhaps more than a century after the writing of Kings. Several generations had passed. By this time, the Babylonian exile ended and many faithful Jews from Judah had now returned to their homeland. God brought them back and was restoring Judah, the seat of David's line, as promised, but they still faced great challenges. The audience of Chronicles was thus a later generation of Israelites, facing somewhat different challenges, in need of a somewhat different message.

Chronicles, then, is the same history of Israel told to a fresh audience that was trying to look forward rather than backward. The books of Kings looked back, using history to explain to its audience what happened to get them to where they were. By contrast, the unknown author(s) of Chronicles used history in order to look ahead, telling this later audience where they should go in the future.

This later audience needed this positive message. Although they had returned from exile, all was not well in God's kingdom. It was no longer independent. Judah had enjoyed political freedom before the exile, but now found itself just an insignificant province in the massive Persian Empire. Not only had it lost independence but also size; the province of Judah after the exile was a fraction of the size it had been before the exile. The Babylonians had lopped off much of Judah's best land and given it to surrounding nations as a punishment to Judah and a reward to these other nations for acting as faithful subjects when Judah had not. Along with controlling little of its former land, Judah also had only a fraction of its former population. Perhaps three-quarters of its numbers had been killed or exiled. Few remained in this smaller version of the earlier Judah.

This later Judah not only dealt with loss of freedom, land, and people, it also faced great financial, social, and religious challenges in trying to rebuild itself. The Babylonians destroyed the infrastructure of the nation during the conquest, leaving those who returned from exile less capable of rebuilding their little province. The society also faced pressure from stronger neighboring societies to assimilate or compromise their culture and religion in ways unacceptable to God. The books of Ezra and Nehemiah record many of the struggles the Israelite society and their leaders faced during this challenging time. Religiously, the Israelites rebuilt their temple, but this symbol of their nation—this point of pride—clearly couldn't measure up to the earlier temple that Solomon had built during a time of great prosperity. Post-exilic Judah had lost much honor and prestige, extremely important aspects for people in that part of the world, both in antiquity and today.

The poorer temple reflected just one of the religious challenges facing the post-exilic Israelite community. Although the nation failed to show faithfulness to their God and had been sent into exile in punishment, the survivors turned from their prior idolatry and were trying to be more faithful. They returned to impoverished Judah as commanded, even though many had enjoyed better situations in exile. They were trying to obey God despite the cost and were looking to God to give them the future he had promised. Even before the exile, God had said that he would eventually restore Israel to a glorious future. He continued to promise this through post-exilic prophets like Haggai and Zechariah, but that glorious future had not yet come to pass.

This community needed hope, and Chronicles was one way that God encouraged them. The book opens with the long section of genealogical information because the nation needed it in several ways. The genealogies connected these people to their more glorious past, reminding them that they were connected to realities greater than what they were currently experiencing.

The genealogies also helped re-form their society. That society was based on familial connections as discussed in the last chapter, and many of those records must have been lost in the turmoil of conquest and exile. Although the modern reader may be bored by the long lists of names at the beginning of the book, the post-exilic Israelites needed them to reestablish who was connected to whom and what rights and responsibilities they had as a result.

In addition to the positive aspects of the genealogies, Chronicles also gave hope by reviewing history in a way that emphasized positive elements rather than negative ones. Kings had highlighted Israel's past failures in order to explain the exile; Chronicles highlighted Israel's past successes to encourage the survivors to move ahead. Although even David and Solomon had failed, this audience didn't need to be reminded of that as much as it needed to be reminded that God had promised that he would send them another David-like leader in the future. They had a glorious past, and their future would recapture at least some of that glory because of a coming chosen and empowered leader. The books of Chronicles encouraged a discouraged people to carry on.

The Goal—What Lessons Did Kings and Chronicles Teach the Israelites?

The preceding paragraphs look at the purposes of Kings and Chronicles and show that both books reviewed Israel's history, but for different purposes. One looked back in order to explain the present to those recently conquered; the other looked back in order to encourage hope for the future in those who had returned from exile—thus the repetition and the differences in the accounts. Beyond these, what else did these two similar but different histories teach their respective audiences? Both showed that God was sovereign over history (even when unpleasant), that he faithfully carried out his purposes over time, and that his people still needed to faithfully fulfill their obligations, even though their circumstances had changed dramatically.

God controls history, even when it's bad

The books of Kings and Chronicles recorded the preceding four centuries of the histories of Israel and Judah, which covered a very tumultuous period in that part of the world. At the beginning of that time, no great powers exercised regional dominance as Egypt had done for so many centuries prior. This gave smaller nations like Israel the chance to rise to greatness, as Israel did under David's leadership. Eventually that era ended and power shifted. The new superpowers now came from Mesopotamia to the east, and the nations of Assyria, Babylon, and Persia took turns dominating the region. Kings and Chronicles showed that God controlled these dramatic international shifts of power and used them for his purposes.

Israel's God controlled history, even when that history did not benefit Israel. It probably would have been much easier for an Israelite to trust in God's sovereignty when David was conquering the region or Solomon was ruling it. It probably got harder to see that same sovereignty when Israel lost its dominance and never regained it. It was probably especially hard to see that sovereignty when Israel not only lost its greatness but its independence altogether and most of its land and people. Nonetheless, the biblical historians showed through Kings and Chronicles that God still ruled in history, even when that history meant some very bad things for God's people.

God carries out his purposes

Just as God controlled history, so he directed it to accomplish his purposes. It had been his purpose to create a people of Israel, give them the land of Canaan, and then raise them to greatness because of the faithfulness of those who led them. Because of the subsequent failures of the people of Israel, both among the leaders and the people as a whole, God's purposes shifted to reducing their nation's power and size, and eventually expelling them from their land. Though painful, God carried out his purposes for his people.

Fortunately God's purposes then shifted toward a much more positive future. He brought them back to their land, and by the time Chronicles was written, he was promising a positive future for them once again. Though the future may not have looked bright, given God's record in fulfilling his purposes in the past, the Israelites should have been able to trust him to carry out his future plans as well. Their history showed through many centuries that God did what he said he would do, and they should have no reason to think that he would do less in the future.

The Israelites needed to remain faithful

The Israelites who received the books of Kings and Chronicles had these records of God's covenantal faithfulness and were called to covenantal faithfulness in return. Eventually God would establish a New Covenant, but until then, they needed to remain faithful to what God had shown them up to that point.

The Benefit—What Can We Learn From the Kings/ Chronicles Repeat?

Beyond appreciating how Kings and Chronicles were directed toward the needs of their original audiences, what modern applications do these books have for today? Just as they showed God's control to their original audiences, so they use that same truth to teach relevant lessons in our day.

God is still sovereign over history—good and bad, large and small

Part of the beauty of Kings and Chronicles was that they could lay out centuries of history for the Israelites of their time. Those people could see how God had directed their nation's history over a very long period of time, and through both good and bad events.

This is no less true in our situation today. Though we don't always have histories as complete and theologically oriented as the ancient Israelites had with Kings and Chronicles, we have even more history to survey and see God's control. The Israelites could track God's sovereign direction over centuries; we can track it over millennia. We can look back over Israelite history in the Bible, and add to that the history of the church after the close of the New Testament. God has an even longer track record with us now than he did at the time of Kings and Chronicles, and it reflects his sovereignty.

As we look back over this increasingly long history of God's work, we, like Israel before us, can see both the good and the bad. We see where God has blessed his people and made them great, and we see other times when things were much more difficult. Just as God controls the good, so he controls the bad, both for ancient Israel and for modern Christians.

This divine control works on both macro and micro levels. God controls the histories and paths of nations, and he controls the histories and paths of individual people. I personally take great comfort in this reality. As I survey God's control over history and nations, it reminds me that he must be exercising similar control over my world. The God who directs nations can easily direct individual destinies. Though many things in my world are beyond my control, they cannot be beyond God's control. I tend to lose sight of that truth, but that doesn't make it less true. The God who shaped the world of ancient Israel just as surely and easily shapes my world today.

God faithfully fulfills his purposes for his people, who need to remain faithful

God does shape the world today as he knows is best, and he does it to carry out his purposes. Honestly, sometimes I can see that, but other times I cannot. I find it easier to trust in God's sovereignty when things go well for me, my family, my ministry, my church, and my nation. But when something goes awry in one of those areas, it's harder to trust God's control. The worst is when something terrible happens—an accident of some kind, or a natural disaster, or a man-made disaster caused by someone's sin. How does God's control show through those things? Well, as we see in histories like Kings and Chronicles, God uses even those things to fulfill his purposes. Those things may not *be* good, but God *uses them for good*. That was true in the days of Kings and Chronicles, and continues to be true today.

God's control provides great comfort for his people since he uses everything for good. But note carefully that the promises regarding God bringing about good expect that we do our part. For example, the famous passage in Romans says, "In all things God works for the good of those who love him, who have been called *according to his purpose*" (Romans 8:28, emphasis added). God will do his part to use even bad things for good, but *we need to be following God's purposes as well*. In the Old Testament this was usually called covenantal fidelity. Today it includes submitting ourselves to God's will and offering ourselves to him (Romans 12:1). If we are committed to doing God's work, he makes sure that everything works out for good.

Conclusion

The books of Kings and Chronicles indeed are repetitious. Though they had distinct purposes for their original audiences, much of that difference is lost on modern readers who don't know the original settings of the books. Once we dig enough to understand those contexts, we should be able to put up with the repetition a little bit better and appreciate what those books taught their original audiences.

When we do, we can see that in one important respect, not much has changed. We as God's people today still need to understand God's control over history and trust him even when things don't work out well. We also need to faithfully follow what he has called us to do. If we do, as the saying goes, "It's all good." God uses everything for his good ends.

In the next chapter we will examine the book of Ecclesiastes—where Solomon, the apparent author, is having a very bad day. The book is dark and pessimistic, almost to the point of seeming unbiblical. What's the deal there? Why is it so gloomy and what is God saying through that book? When you're ready, let's turn and discuss that rather negative and challenging part of the Bible.

Study Questions

1. Do you enjoy reading the history of the Israelite kings as told in Kings? Why or why not?

2. According to this chapter, who was the original audience for 1 and 2 Kings, and what were the main reasons the author wrote these books? What did he want his audience to learn?

3. According to this chapter, who was the original audience for 1 and 2 Chronicles, and what were the main reasons the author wrote these books? What did he want his audience to learn?

4. Is it still true today that God is faithful and sovereign over the histories of nations and individuals, and wants his people to remain faithful to him? Is that difficult for you to remember and believe? If so, what makes it hard?

7

Why Is Ecclesiastes So Dark and Gloomy?

The Problem—Why Is Ecclesiastes So Negative?

Nestled in the midst of several positive, constructive, poetic books in the Old Testament, we find the surprisingly dark and gloomy book of Ecclesiastes. When we first look at the book of Psalms, we find that although a number of psalms deal with the pains of life, the majority praise God for how great he is and for the wonderful things he has done. Thus, that poetic book feels rather positive. Proverbs then follows, describing the benefits of wisdom and giving advice on how to live a godly, fruitful life—again, quite constructive. Then comes the melancholy book of Ecclesiastes, after which we have the Song of Solomon—a beautiful, powerfully erotic book full of poetic images that extols the beauties of love and physical intimacy.

So in the midst of these positive books we have Ecclesiastes, where the author seems to be having a *very* bad day, or maybe a very bad *life*. Parts of the book are so negative that sometimes they sound like they don't belong in the Bible. The repeated phrase "All is vanity" (or "Everything is meaningless") can't be true, can it? Doesn't knowing God give life meaning? Why, then, would the author say that everything is meaningless, or any of the other pessimistic things in this book? What was he trying to say, and what can we learn from it today?

The dark tone of Ecclesiastes is actually just one of a number of problems I find associated with the book. The other issues are as follows:

What does the title Ecclesiastes mean?

The very title of the book is problematic. The term *Ecclesiastes* appears in an English dictionary only as the title for this biblical book, so the English title doesn't tell us much. The title is actually a transliteration (writing the same word using the closest corresponding letters from another language) of the Greek word *Ekklēsiastēs,* which translates the Hebrew title *qohelet. Qohelet* is an uncommon Hebrew term referring to the speaker or author of Ecclesiastes. It appears only a few times in the Bible, and only in this single book. In other words, the book's title is an obscure term. The word is actually related to the Hebrew word for "assembly," so the word *may* mean something like "teacher" or "preacher" (see 1:1), as in one who spoke to an assembly of people. Whatever this difficult term means, it stands for the person who spoke or wrote the words in this book.

Who wrote Ecclesiastes?

Along with the title, the identity of the book's author is also somewhat problematic. At first glance, the text seems to clearly imply that Solomon, son of King David, wrote the book. After all, the very first verse describes the author as "the son of David, king in Jerusalem." That clearly fits Solomon, as do the subsequent statements of his great wisdom, wealth, possessions, and pleasures (1:16; 2:7–8). All of this seems to fit Solomon, and for centuries the traditional understanding of the book assumed that Solomon was the author.

However, the book never states outright that Solomon wrote it, and the phrase "son of David" *could* mean someone besides Solomon. As we might naturally assume, the Hebrew word for "son" usually means a first generation male offspring. But *son* also has other meanings; it can mean a later physical descendant as well. For example, Jesus and his father Joseph were descendants of David many generations down the line, and the New Testament rightly calls both of them "son of David" (Matthew 1:1, 20). So a son of David who ruled in Jerusalem (Ecclesiastes 1:1) could describe *any* Davidic king who reigned in the 400-plus years of Judah's history that followed King David.

In addition, the author's claim that he "increased in wisdom more than anyone who has ruled over Jerusalem before me" (1:16) sounds a bit strange if it came from Solomon. Only two kings of Israel ruled before Solomon—Saul and David—and of those, only David ruled in Jerusalem. Would Solomon really make such a claim when referring only to his father? It seems strange and sounds more like something a later king might say.

On the other hand, could any king—besides Solomon—make the claims that we find in the book—claims of unsurpassed wisdom and wealth and accomplishment? That would also seem strange, perhaps even more so. Thus, the matter of the book's authorship is also uncertain. All things considered, the book does seem to come from Solomon's perspective, though *maybe* it is being presented through a wise teacher *portraying himself as Solomon*. I would compare this idea to attending a modern presentation by "Mark Twain." If I went to a performance by Mark Twain, I would expect someone dressed and made to look like Mark Twain, who would say things like he would have said. *Maybe* this is what we have with Ecclesiastes—someone presenting himself like Solomon, and the original audience would have understood this as we would understand a presentation by "Mark Twain." So whether these words come from Solomon (most likely), or someone presenting himself as Solomon, we are hearing from a wise person very disillusioned with life and searching for meaning.

Why is the author so negative?

Regardless of whether we are reading the words of Solomon or not, this inspired author is saying some negative things that don't seem to fit very well with the rest of the Bible. For example, the book of Proverbs, written largely by Solomon (note Proverbs 1:1 and 10:1, but also 30:1 and 31:1 for other authors), repeatedly extols the benefits of wisdom. The author of Ecclesiastes, by contrast, laments the limits of wisdom and says that a wise man is no better than a fool (2:15–16). Those ideas don't seem to match Proverbs or the rest of the Bible. In addition, the author generally comes across as a severe skeptic about many things, emphasizing the futility of life, or at least the futility of life lived apart from God.

Even the theme of the book is negative, as shown in the initial phrase, "Vanity of vanities." This kind of expression is the way the Hebrews would express a superlative. A superlative expresses the *most* of something. A superlative denotes more than a simple quality (like good), and even more than a comparative (better); a superlative is that quality to the extreme (best). The Hebrews expressed a superlative by saying "something of something," to express the *most* of that quality or idea. For example, they would say "king of kings" to describe the most powerful king, or "Holy of Holies" to designate the holiest part of the temple. The author of Ecclesiastes uses "vanity of vanities" to express the rather negative thought that life is entirely vain or completely meaningless. Really? Isn't that a bit exaggerated?

Along with the negative theme, the author expresses numerous other pessimistic thoughts. For example, in 2:23 he writes, "All their days their work is grief and pain; even at night their minds do not rest. This too is meaningless." Is life *really* that bad? Surely life brings some pain and grief, but not *all* days. And life is *not* meaningless, though it may seem that way at times. Ecclesiastes has many such negative, exaggerated statements. Why do we find this dark book in the Bible?

Don't statements in the book contradict themselves?

Along with negative elements that appear to contradict other teachings in the Bible, some statements in Ecclesiastes appear to contradict other things in the same book! For example, in 2:10, 24, the author notes how good it is to find pleasure in one's work: "My heart took delight in all my labor, and this was the reward for all my toil" (v. 10); "A person can do nothing better than to eat and drink and find satisfaction in their own toil. This too, I see, is from the hand of God" (v. 24). But between those two statements, he seems to argue the opposite when he says, "What do people get for all the toil and anxious striving with which they labor under the sun? . . . This too is meaningless" (22–23). Why both positive and negative?

We see from these examples that elements of Ecclesiastes are obscure, negative, and seemingly contradictory. Those sound like characteristics of poor literature to me, not characteristics of a divinely inspired book. What are they doing in the Bible? We find the answers to some of these questions when we analyze the book's genre (type of literature), as we will do in our next section.

The Style—What Kind of Literature Is Ecclesiastes?

Ecclesiastes is a good example of ancient Near Eastern *wisdom literature*. This is a genre of literature well known from the world of the Bible, both from Israel and from nearby peoples. The cultures of Egypt and Babylon, for example, also produced wisdom literature, in which a wise person would seek to instruct his audience (often cast as a younger man) about God, life, and how to live virtuously.

Wisdom literature often took one of two forms. The first, *proverbial wisdom,* is written in the form of proverbs, which are short, expressive, memorable statements giving practical advice on how to live well. The biblical book of Proverbs obviously fits this type of wisdom literature, and includes sayings like "When pride comes, then comes disgrace, but with humility comes wisdom" (11:2). A more modern example of a proverb would be "Don't cry over spilled milk," which teaches that we can't undo something that has already happened, so we best accept it and move on. Proverbs from the Bible and from other cultures teach about life and how to live it through concise and instructive sayings.

The second type of wisdom literature is more philosophical and seeks to explore the bigger questions of life. For example, the book of Job deals with the troubling question "Why do innocent people suffer?" and is cast in the form of a dialogue between Job and several of his friends. Ecclesiastes gives us the other obvious biblical example of this philosophical wisdom literature. This book is a monologue, and has the author wrestling with the question "What is the meaning of life?"

These types of literature are often written in poetic fashion. Note the use of short lines, often written in pairs where the second line restates the first, or states the opposite of the first. Because this literature is poetic, it often bears the characteristics of poetry, including hyperbole or exaggeration. We'll discuss this more thoroughly in the next chapter on prophecy, another genre often written in poetic style. Poetry is a challenging genre to understand, especially if you are reading poetry from a different culture. Exaggeration from our world is fairly easy to recognize—"I had to stop at *a hundred red lights* on my way to the meeting"—but less so coming from a different culture.

Thus, the frequent statement in Ecclesiastes "All is vanity!" or "Everything is meaningless!" doesn't have to be *literally* true. It's likely an exaggeration in which the author is emphasizing how futile everything *seems,* at least from time to time.

Clearly life does seem futile at times, so if we can allow the author of Ecclesiastes to exaggerate, we can accept that he is speaking hyperbolically about his frustration with life—at least on that day. Ecclesiastes makes more sense and fits better into the context of the whole Bible when we dial back some of the statements and interpret them as exaggerations describing frustrations in life.

Another key point to remember when interpreting Ecclesiastes is that the author, be it Solomon or whoever, is trying to make sense of life from *a pre-Christian perspective*. We read and analyze his words from the perspective of a much later time period, already knowing what God would later reveal through Jesus and the New Testament. God has revealed truth to humans progressively—Abraham and Moses knew God well, but God didn't show them all the theological truths that would become clear through the New Testament. Abraham and Moses didn't understand heaven and resurrection and so on like we do, nor did the author of Ecclesiastes. He was wrestling with the meaning of life and things like why wise people die just as fools do, and he couldn't yet understand how eternal life would help make sense of such issues. For him, life basically ended at the grave, and not everything was sorted out by that time. We understand that now, and know that God will finish making things right after death, but the author of Ecclesiastes wasn't aware of that truth. We need to read his struggles in light of the *earlier theological framework* from which he was writing.

Ecclesiastes is an ancient Near Eastern piece of wisdom literature that wrestled with the big question of how to make sense of life, and it did so before God revealed all that we as Christians today understand from the New Testament.

No wonder some of what the author said doesn't seem to land on the correct runway; he was trying to fly a much older airplane without the advantage of modern navigational instruments. As we seek to understand what the author of Ecclesiastes was saying, let's give him some leeway and appreciate how well he did fly his more primitive airplane given the circumstances.

The Goal—What Lessons Did (and Does) Ecclesiastes Teach?

So what did the author of Ecclesiastes teach his original audience, and what nuggets can we find hidden in plain sight in this dark—and somewhat exaggerated—yet inspired book? I suggest the following:

Life is cyclical, and different things are appropriate at different times

As I have grown older, I have noticed that some things are good or bad (or both), but they occur in a natural cycle of life. The birth of a child is a wonderful thing, and death is a sad thing, but both are part of what happens to all humans. Most people go through the cycle in which they are born, grow, experience good and bad, and eventually their bodies wear out and they die. Some of those experiences are terrific and some are profoundly sad, but that's the way life is. The author of Ecclesiastes understood this and expressed this idea in timeless, poetic style at the beginning of chapter 3: "There is a time for everything, and a season for every activity under heaven: a time to be born and a time to die, a time to plant and a time to uproot, a time to kill and a time to heal." An

American songwriter used these words in a song from the 1960s called "Turn! Turn! Turn!"[1]

Why would a (relatively) modern, rather secular musician use words written perhaps 3,000 years ago? Because this songwriter recognized that *Qohelet* was correct when he described how cyclical life is and how different things are appropriate at different times. Indeed, dancing is appropriate at times, but mourning is appropriate at other times. Sometimes we need to build and establish, and other times we need to tear down. Sometimes we need to speak up, and other times it's better to remain silent and listen. Life is like that. The author of Ecclesiastes understood this and wrote about it, and an American musician repeated his words in a more updated fashion. Life is cyclical, and different occasions call for different actions.

Often life isn't fair

In addition to describing how life is cyclical and varied, the author of Ecclesiastes noted that oftentimes life just isn't fair (9:11). We all see that and notice how the lack of fairness manifests in different ways. For example, fairness would mean that people who do what is right should prosper while bad people should suffer, and that's often the case. But not always; sometimes the reverse happens (7:15), and it isn't fair. In another example, some people are the "haves"—they have money, power, fame, or whatever. Others are the "have-nots," and they can't make many things in life work as well as the haves. Sometimes people are haves because they have earned

---

1. Pete Seeger, "Turn! Turn! Turn! (To Everything There Is a Season)," 1962. The Byrds' 1965 version became an international hit.

it; other times people work just as hard but don't get it for some reason. It's not fair, but that's the way it is.

As much as I appreciate the American justice system, I also notice a lack of fairness in it. We sometimes portray our ideal of justice with the statue entitled "Lady Justice." This figure holds a balanced scale in one hand and a sword in the other. These symbolize how a proper system of justice should weigh things appropriately and fairly (the balanced scale), and also have the power to carry out proper penalties (the sword). In addition to the scale and sword, Lady Justice often wears a blindfold. Justice is blind, or at least should be, to whomever is being judged. It shouldn't matter if the person being judged is a have or a have-not, but it often does. I see that the haves can afford better lawyers, and they often can manipulate the legal system to get the desired ruling. It's not fair, but that's the way it often is.

The author of Ecclesiastes saw this same reality, even though he lived in a society with a legal system very different from ours. He described the advantages of the haves over the have-nots by saying, "I saw the tears of the oppressed—and they have no comforter; power was on the side of their oppressors—and they have no comforter. And I declared that the dead, who had already died, are happier than the living, who are still alive. But better than both is he who has never been born, who has not seen the evil that is done under the sun" (4:1–3). Again, dialing back some of the exaggeration, *Qohelet* says that the haves take advantage of the have-nots, and sometimes there's nothing that the have-nots can do about it on this side of the grave. It's not fair, but that's the way life is sometimes.

Many things in life promise satisfaction but don't deliver

In addition to describing how unfair life is at times, the author of Ecclesiastes noted well how we pursue some things in life because we think they will give us satisfaction, but they ultimately don't. This part of the book in particular sounds like it comes from Solomon, because the author says that he tried many things that we know Solomon tried, but found them unsatisfying.

For one thing, the author wrote, "Whoever loves money never has money enough; whoever loves wealth is never satisfied with their income. This too is meaningless" (5:10). If you are like me, you might say that you don't *love* money, but you do *like* it. You like it enough to want a little more than what you have now, and think that if you just had *a little more,* you would be happy. *Qohelet* says that's not true. Those who want money won't be satisfied with a little more, or even a lot more.

Perhaps the best illustration of this comes from a quote ascribed to John D. Rockefeller, the nineteenth-century American oil magnate. Rockefeller became America's first billionaire and, when adjusted for inflation, the richest man who has ever lived. Someone reportedly asked Rockefeller how much money was enough, to which he replied, "Just one dollar more." A person may be as rich as Solomon or John D. Rockefeller, but however much money he has, it isn't enough. Money is powerful, but it just doesn't satisfy.

The author of Ecclesiastes also wrote that he pursued satisfaction through pleasure (including sex), laughter, alcohol, and accomplishments, but none of these satisfied. "I denied myself nothing my eyes desired; I refused my heart no pleasure. . . . Yet when I surveyed all that my hands had done and what I had toiled to achieve, everything was meaningless, a chasing after the wind; nothing was gained under the sun" (2:10–11). Again, allowing for exaggeration, this man who had so much said that none of it gave him the satisfaction that he craved. Sad, isn't it?

Certain things in life do satisfy

Despite the pessimistic perspective just discussed, *Qohelet* did say that some things are good and that we *should* find pleasure in them. Like what? Like enjoying work, for one thing (2:24–25; 8:15). We all understand that work gets frustrating at times. After all, the penalty for the first man's sin was a curse on his realm of work (Genesis 3:17–19). Since then, all work has had its form of "thorns and thistles," but God gave humans work even before the fall (Genesis 2:15), and work is essentially good. Assuming we are in a suitable type of employment, work is essentially good, and *Qohelet* urges us to enjoy it.

He also urges us to enjoy other things like life, human relationships, possessions, and food and drink (5:19; 9:7–10). God has provided for our needs, and if we are at peace with God, we should also be able to find pleasure in these important but sometimes mundane and challenging parts of life. Though they will not give us ultimate satisfaction, they should provide pleasure.

The author of Ecclesiastes saves the most important of these satisfying elements for the end of the book. After working through chapter after chapter describing so many things that *don't* give promised satisfaction and meaning (as well as a few that do), he says, "Here is the conclusion of the matter: Fear God and keep his commandments, for this is the duty of all mankind. For God will bring every deed into judgment, including every hidden thing, whether it is good or evil" (12:13–14). Ultimate meaning comes only from being rightly related to the God who will judge everyone in the end. We need to relate to him properly ("fear God"), and then live accordingly ("keep his commandments"). Indeed, this is the conclusion of the search for meaning in life.

Conclusion

It's really pretty simple. Know God and do what he asks of you. Modern believers living after the New Testament and the ministry of Jesus would probably describe this principle differently. Perhaps we would use words like "Trust in the death of Jesus to make you right with a holy God, and then live as God asks of us in the New Testament." Though we might phrase it differently than the author of Ecclesiastes did, the heart of the matter is still the same. If we aren't rightly related to God, none of these other things like money or pleasure will give us what we need. But if we *are* rightly related to God, then our eternity is secure, and things in this life like work and relationships and even food are pleasures for us to enjoy *now*.

Next, we turn to books written by prophets—God's spokesmen who brought messages of warning, judgment, and hope. The prophets primarily warned God's people of their covenantal mistakes and explained God's direction for history. Some of them wrote books, and those books can be difficult to understand for various reasons. Let's see if we can sort out what was happening in the books of prophecy and what we can learn from them.

Study Questions

1. What are your impressions of Ecclesiastes? Why?

2. Do you think the author of Ecclesiastes was exaggerating to make a point when he said, "Everything is meaningless?" If so, what point might he have been making—what was he saying?

3. Would you agree with the points made in this chapter that life is cyclical? That life often isn't fair? That many things in life promise satisfaction but few deliver?

4. Do you have God at the core of your life? Do you know him and do you walk with him? If so, are you able to enjoy things like relationships, possessions, even food?

8

What on Earth Are the Prophets Talking About?

The Problem—What Are the Prophets Saying?

The prophets of the Old Testament acted as spokesmen for God and played a major role in Israelite culture. This influence is recorded and reflected in our Bibles. A large part of the Old Testament—16[1] of the 39 books—consists of specifically prophetic books, and the prophets' influence extends well beyond these particular books. We saw in our earlier chapter on Kings and Chronicles that those books include material about a number of prophets, and the historical material itself was written with a prophetic outlook. So by the time the modern reader of the Bible gets to the

---

1. Christian Bibles have seventeen books in the section of Prophets, but this number includes the book of Lamentations, apparently placed there because of its assumed authorship by the prophet Jeremiah. Since Lamentations is clearly a lament rather than a book of prophecy, one can say the Bible contains sixteen rather than seventeen books of prophecy.

books of prophecy (Isaiah–Malachi), many of the biblical prophets will already be familiar. Since these prophets were often interesting characters who did and said things in dramatic ways, their books are frequently vivid and piercing. Often, unfortunately, their colorful and penetrating words lose much of their impact for the modern reader because we can't understand them.

It's not just modern readers who have difficulty with the works of these gentlemen (some women also served as prophets, but none of the books of prophecy had female authors, as far as we know). Five hundred years ago, the reformer Martin Luther admitted that he had similar difficulty. And Luther wasn't a typical churchman. Luther was a doctor of theology, an accomplished professor of theology, and an expositor of Scripture whose works are still read today. So it's not insignificant that even Martin Luther lamented that prophets "have a queer way of talking, like people who, instead of proceeding in an orderly manner, ramble off from one thing to the next so that you cannot make head or tail of them or see what they are getting at."[2] One of my students stated this problem more succinctly: "What on earth are the prophets talking about?"

I have often wondered the very same thing. The prophetic material is often colorful and of course inspired, but it can be terribly difficult to follow and thus learn anything from it. As I have read, studied, and taught the prophetic books over the years, I have identified at least four reasons for these challenges:

2. *Works*, Weimar, ed., 19:350, cited in Gerhard von Rad, *Old Testament Theology* (Edinburgh, Scotland: Oliver & Boyd, 1965), 2:33, no. 1.

1. Prophetic material is often poetic, and poetry can be very difficult to understand

The Bible contains two main kinds of literature—narrative and poetry. Narrative (like the majority of Kings and Chronicles) typically flows more naturally and smoothly, and is written in paragraph form. It is straightforward and intuitive to interpret, since it consists mostly of stories. Poetry, by contrast, is written in a different style that is easy to recognize but more challenging to interpret. Poetry is typically written using shorter lines that don't reach to the margins of the page and are often grouped in stanzas. Although not all the material in the prophetic books is poetic, much of it is, and you can see that by the way the text is laid out on the page.

Poetic material is difficult to interpret, largely because it uses so many figures of speech. The authors don't make statements in a direct manner, but rather say things using metaphors and other literary devices. For example, the poet doesn't say, "God provides security," but rather, "God *is a rock*." God isn't *literally* a rock, of course, but it's more powerful and memorable to say something that doesn't quite work on a literal level. This mismatch makes the reader think about what the author is saying, since it is more striking and easier to remember. Poetry can be more powerful than prose as long as we understand the poetic figures. If we don't, it loses its impact. Unfortunately, that's what happens for many modern readers when they read the books of prophecy. The meaning of the figures gets lost, so the reader does as well.

Poetry is also harder to interpret than narrative because it uses hyperbole (exaggeration). We often use hyperbole when we speak: "I've told you *a million times* not to do that!" Such a statement is obviously untrue, but the speaker overstates the point to make it more forceful. Usually we recognize modern exaggerations, since we probably know the speaker and/or the situation well enough to understand that the statement can't literally be true.

But when we read poetry from a very different context, we may or may not catch the exaggeration. For example, it's fairly obvious that the psalmist is overstating his distress when he says, "All night long I flood my bed with weeping and drench my couch with tears" (6:6), since no one cries *that* much. But is Isaiah also exaggerating when he says, "Every valley shall be raised up, every mountain and hill made low" (40:4) when God appears? Will God literally change the very uneven landscape east of Jerusalem, or is this a hyperbolic way of saying that when God comes to Jerusalem, it will be a truly magnificent occasion? Since the prophets lived and spoke in a different world some 2,500 years ago, it's sometimes hard to know just what they meant.

I think figures and exaggerations can be more problematic for readers who believe that the Bible is inspired and thus true. If the Bible is true, then wouldn't it be true as stated? Shouldn't we trust that God and the authors meant what they said and how they said it? Well, yes and no. Yes, the Bible is true, but it may well use true *figures of speech* and thus not be true on a literal level. For example, it is true that God is in control, but if a poet says God is "enthroned," that may not mean that God literally sits in a chair. The throne may simply be a symbol of authority and power. Such figures (and, by extension, poetry) can be true, but in a different way than we may read them at first. This poetic characteristic makes prophetic material tricky to understand. We may need to question whether the prophets are speaking literally or using some figure of speech.

2. We may not understand because we have lost the original cultural context

Along with interpreting figures and exaggeration, we also must understand prophetic material in context. I teach my students that prophets were the preachers of their time. They gave God's words and perspective on situations, and they encouraged people to live accordingly. Though not inspired in the same way, today's preachers do much the same. When I sit and listen to modern preachers, I rarely have trouble understanding them. If I don't know the preachers personally, I usually still know enough of the world from which they draw their illustrations that I can follow what they are saying without difficulty.

I imagine the same was true with the prophets in their day. Their audiences probably had little trouble tracking with them, since the audience either knew the prophet or knew enough of the common culture to grasp what the prophets were getting at. It's the jump from that culture to ours that creates problems when we read the prophets today.

We don't always find their works difficult, since some figures work rather well regardless of the time. Saying, "God is a rock" is clear because most people intuitively know to associate *rock* with ideas of strength and security. However, when you read that the prophet Isaiah said Israel had become "like a hut in a cucumber field" (Isaiah 1:8), that meaning may be lost. Most people in our world aren't familiar with fields of cucumbers and the flimsy temporary shelters that Middle Eastern workers, both ancient and modern, would build and use for the few weeks of intensive work at harvest time. Thus, the meaning and power of Isaiah's figure of speech can easily get lost. The prophetic books contain hundreds of such figures that no longer communicate effectively to our world and cultural context.

3. We may not understand because we have lost the original historical context

Just as we can miss the meaning of texts because of a difference in cultures, so we can miss the point if we can't anchor the text historically. Again, when I listen to a modern preacher, I don't have to think about a reference to some current event. I am usually aware of the major events and understand references to them. But when I read a text from a different time period, I may or may not know what events the text is referring to. For example, the prophet Nahum refers to the fall of the major Egyptian city of Thebes (Nahum 3:8) to warn the Assyrian city of Nineveh that it would fall as well. Someone in Nahum's world would probably have easily understood his reference. But if I have never heard of the place, or if I know about it but don't know that Thebes fell to the Assyrians in 663 BC, Nahum's use of Thebes to warn Nineveh (which would fall in 612 BC) has little or no impact.

Learning the historical context proves helpful when exploring ancient material like the books of the biblical prophets. Understanding context can take a bit of work, but usually makes the text much clearer and more interesting. Sometimes, though, we can't recover the context no matter how hard we try. For example, the prophet Joel wrote to farmers in Judah about an invasion of locusts. This devastating event apparently foreshadowed an even worse event—God using an invading army to judge Judah. Though we can understand that idea in general, Joel's specific context eludes us. We don't know when Joel spoke or when the locusts invaded. We don't even know if the locusts were real or figurative. Farmers would understand the devastation caused by locusts whether real or not, so the illustration would be effective, even if not literally true. But we don't know when the locusts came, if they did. Thus we can't be certain about which army would come either. Joel's audience, though, would have known if locusts had really come and understood his warning clearly. We don't know for sure what happened and when Joel preached, so we struggle to grasp his entire meaning.

4. We may not understand because we aren't familiar with the theological context

The importance of context applies to theological matters as well. As we discussed in the chapter on Kings and Chronicles, the Israelites of the Old Testament were living under the Mosaic Covenant, which guided their relationship with God. We also noted that Christians today are under the New Covenant. Many aspects of the Mosaic Covenant have carried through to the New Covenant, so we intuitively understand much of what guided the ancient Israelites. Some things, though, have changed, and those changes can confuse the modern reader of the Bible.

The prophets called their hearers to live according to the Mosaic Covenant, and their audience understood what they should do. Modern readers may not know what in the prophetic messages is applicable in today's world—and what is not. For example, it's easy to see that we should refrain from theft, acts of injustice or immorality, and so on. But should we still sacrifice animals (probably not, because of Jesus' sacrifice), make pilgrimages to Jerusalem, fast, or even tithe? Were those solely for ancient Israelites under the Mosaic Covenant, or do they still apply to Christians under the New Covenant today? Sometimes understanding what *was* required but no longer applies gets really tricky. And that often comes into play with the messages of the prophets. Those ancient preachers called their hearers to do certain things, and modern readers can get confused about what is still relevant and what is not.

All of these issues—the poetic figures and the cultural, historical, and theological contexts—frequently make it difficult for the modern reader to understand and apply the messages of the biblical prophets. These issues can make us wonder what on earth the prophets were talking about, and if those books have *anything* useful to say to our world. Well, they do. The prophetic books *do* have valuable messages, even for our rather different world, but we have to do some groundwork first to appreciate what they said. We need to understand the purposes of the prophetic messages, develop a useful strategy for interpreting the prophets, and gain a relatively clear idea of what the prophets have to say to our world.

The Goal—What Purposes Did the Prophets and Their Messages Serve?

To help us figure out what the prophets were talking about, let's first discuss the general functions of the prophets and their messages. Understanding these in a broad way should help us as we try to sort out what specific prophets or their prophetic messages were saying.

Intermediaries Between God and People

Prophets primarily functioned as intermediaries between the divine and human worlds. Although many people today wrestle with whether or not they believe God exists, such was not an issue in the biblical world. Israelites, as well as peoples around them, assumed that there was a God, or gods, and that god(s) affected life in this world. Their challenge was to figure out what the god(s) wanted and how to influence them, if possible. Many cultures at the time had prophets, and all these prophets acted as go-betweens for communicating with the divine world.

The Israelites had prophets as did the nearby cultures, but Israel's prophets differed from the others in certain ways. The biggest differences were the character of the god(s) the prophets represented and what standards the gods set for their people. The God of Israel had (and has) a perfectly moral character, unlike the gods of surrounding peoples. Israel's God held his people to a correspondingly higher moral standard as well. He not only wanted his people to serve him, he expected them to live in a way that reflected his standards, which benefitted them as well.

God often communicated his standards through the prophets to their human audience, which might consist of the entire Israelite nation, a group, or a particular individual (often the king, because he had so much influence in the culture). God might also speak through the prophet to people outside of the Israelite community, such as the nation of Edom (in the book of Obadiah) or a person such as Hazael, the future Aramean king (2 Kings 8:7–15).

Reminders of Covenantal Obligations

The Israelites were bound to a covenantal relationship with a single, moral God, and Israelite prophets communicated on behalf of that God, Yahweh, to his people. As prophets gave their messages that connected people with God, usually they spoke about covenantal obligations. The Israelites needed to follow the laws and teachings given with the Mosaic Covenant (discussed in an earlier chapter), but usually they weren't doing a very good job. The prophets spoke for God, usually reminding the Israelites of their failings within the covenant—obviously a rather difficult and challenging task. People who fail don't like to be reminded of that and typically resent the ones who point it out.

Doers of Miracles and Predictors of the Future

The prophets faithfully fulfilled their difficult, unpopular work, but God sometimes helped them by giving them the ability to do miraculous work. Since the Israelites often didn't want to listen to prophets, God enabled them to do miracles or predict the future as a way of proving that the prophets were indeed speaking for God. This showed that the people really did need to heed their messages.

We see this promise of enablement starting with Moses before Israel even became a nation. When God first called Moses to return to Egypt to free his people, he also gave him miraculous abilities—like turning a rod into a snake and changing water to blood—as proof of his authentic calling (Exodus 4:1–9). Years later, the prophet Elijah would validate his calling by miraculously raising a dead child to life (1 Kings 17:22–24). Many years after that, Jesus would authenticate his prophetic calling with a similar miracle (Luke 7:11–16).

Likewise, prophets could often predict the future as a way of confirming their identity and ministry. This form of proof also started with Moses, who told the Israelites how to recognize a true prophet: "If what a prophet proclaims in the name of the Lord does not take place or come true, that is a message the Lord has not spoken. That prophet has spoken presumptuously" (Deuteronomy 18:22). False and true prophets would arise in Israel in the future, and the true prophets would distinguish themselves by performing miracles and accurately predicting future events.

Motivate Covenantal Faithfulness

The prophets did all these things—mediate between human and divine worlds, remind about covenantal obligations, perform miracles, and predict the future—so that their audience would listen to God's words and do what he asked. God wanted them to live according to what they had promised in the Mosaic Covenant, although he knew they ultimately would refuse and he would have to punish them with conquest and exile. But even when those terrible things happened, God didn't cease speaking to the Israelites. He continued to send his prophets during and after the exile. These later prophets pointed out that the Israelites deserved the punishment they had received, but that better days were ahead. God would restore Israel, so it was not too late for them to demonstrate faithfulness. The exile and return had made life much more difficult, but God had not abandoned them. They, in return, should finally manifest proper faithfulness, and overall, they did much better after the exile.

The Process—How Do We Interpret the Prophets?

Once we appreciate who the prophets were and what they sought to accomplish through their messages, we still need to know what to do with the prophetic books when we read them now. Appreciating the original purposes is one thing, but it's even more important to figure out how God can still speak through those ancient messages to us and our modern world. So how do we do that?

Learn the Context of the Genre and the Book

As the preceding sections discussed, knowing the context of the prophets is helpful in understanding their books. We need to understand the prophets generally, and I tried to describe the major aspects of that above. Beyond a general understanding, we should also learn the specific context of a particular prophet and his book.

Let's take Jeremiah as an example. Before diving into the book, read up a bit on the prophet and his ministry. What do we know about Jeremiah? When did he live and what was happening in Judah and the broader world at the time? What were his main concerns (i.e., the book's themes)? How is the book structured? (With Jeremiah this is quite difficult, because the book is scrambled chronologically, and we can't figure out when to date some of the messages.) In short, we need to put ourselves in the world of the prophet and his audience as much as possible. We can't do that entirely, but the better we can do it, the more clearly we will interpret what he is saying.

How do we learn the context of a book? Fortunately, we have many biblical study helps available today. A study Bible may have an introduction to the individual sections of the Bible, including the prophets. Reading the introduction should help with the general context. A good study Bible also contains an introduction to each book, such as Jeremiah or Isaiah. The introduction will discuss what is known about the author, audience, themes, structure, significant challenges to understanding the book, etc. Reading the introduction before reading the book will help you to understand and interpret the prophet's words. If you don't wish to use a study Bible, you can also access a Bible dictionary or encyclopedia for articles on books and subjects. Many such study aids are available online as well, but know that some online sources are outdated, and a recently published text may be more useful.

Remember These Principles

After doing some research on the context of the book in order to place yourself in the prophet's world as much as possible, read the prophetic book. Typically prophetic books contain both narrative and poetry. The narrative material tells about events of the time, probably including what happened to the prophet during his ministry. Most of the book, though, likely consists of prophetic messages. I read these as ancient sermons and try to interpret them as messages from ancient preachers to their audience. These messages often contain poetic material, and we need to keep in mind the unique challenges (discussed above) and interpret accordingly. In addition, the following points have helped me understand prophetic poetry in particular:

1. THE MATERIAL MAY BE FIGURATIVE OR CONTEXTUALLY FIGURATIVE

Remember especially that poetic material typically contains many figures, which are true but not always literal. When Isaiah said, "They will beat their swords into plowshares and their spears into pruning hooks" (Isaiah 2:4), he was probably speaking figuratively. Perhaps he did envision people literally remaking military weapons into tools of peace. But more likely, this was a figurative way to say, "Instead of applying themselves to military arts (which most cultures do), the rule of God's anointed leader will be characterized by people practicing peaceful arts instead." Such is a figure.

The prophets may also be *contextually figurative*. By this I mean that the prophet may have used a figure that was meaningful for his culture in his time period, but the reality will take place in a later, perhaps very different culture and context. For example, the figure above about the plowshares and pruning hooks used to confuse me. Since Isaiah referred to ancient weapons in his prophecy, I thought the fulfillment needed to have taken place during the time people used those ancient weapons. This created a disconnect for me. The promised fulfillment hasn't yet come, but militaries don't even use those weapons anymore. How then could the promise come true?

If the prophecy is *contextually figurative,* it will come true at some point regardless of what time or culture the figures are from. The swords, plowshares, and pruning hooks may be outdated, but the prophecy is not. It *will* come true, and when it does, those people will not need to invest time, money, and blood in military matters, regardless of how war will be practiced at the time. It won't matter if they use swords, machine guns, or Star Trek-like phasers, because when the Messiah rules, the world will be at peace instead of war.

2. THE CHRONOLOGY MAY BE UNCLEAR

Just as the contextual setting for the prophetic figures may be unclear, so may the chronology. When God says through his prophets that something will happen, it will. But *when* may be unclear. This gets especially tricky if the prophetic fulfillment has multiple parts. When will they all happen? We may not know. One part may have come true in the prophet's lifetime, another may have occurred centuries later, and another part may still be in the future.

For example, the prophet Malachi predicted that the prophet Elijah would return before the Day of the Lord. (The "Day of the Lord" was a way of saying "when God steps into history to make things right, often with judgment.") When did this take place? According to Jesus, John the Baptist was Elijah (Matthew 11:14), who helped prepare people for Jesus, who literally was God stepping into history. But during his first coming, Jesus didn't complete all of his ministry; he will return to do more. Likewise, John the Baptist didn't fulfill all of the ministry prophesied about Elijah (perhaps the reason for his denial in John 1:21) because he knew there was more to come. Elijah did come in the person of John the Baptist, but he will come again later.

3. THE ACTIONS MAY BE ONGOING OR THEMATIC

The challenges with chronology in the prophetic material reflect another closely related characteristic. The prophets often speak of God doing something that may be *ongoing* or *thematic*. Sometimes they say God will do something, and it happens once and is done. For example, the prophet Micah predicted that God's future ruler would be born in Bethlehem (Micah 5:2), and Jesus was born in Bethlehem (Matthew 2:1–12). Done. The prophecy was finished.

With other prophecies it's not so simple. The prophet may speak of God doing something, and it happens in multiple stages or events. It may be a prophecy with multiple fulfillments at different times, as with Elijah's coming, or the prophet may speak of God doing something that is *characteristic* of God's ongoing actions that are happening all the time. Isaiah prophesied, "In that day they will say, 'Surely this is our God; we trusted in him, and he saved us'" (25:9). When did that happen? Whenever God rescued any of his people from anything, this happened. God did it by rescuing some of the Israelites from death at the time of the exile. He did it again by bringing many of them back to Judah after the exile and rescuing the Jewish people from extinction. He did it again when he made it possible for all humans to be delivered from eternal death through the ministry of Jesus, and this applies to every person when they count on Jesus' death and resurrection to make them right with God. Saving or rescuing people is *characteristic* of God, and the prophets may refer to such an ongoing truth in their messages.

4. GOD'S JUDGMENTS MAY BE CONDITIONAL, EVEN IF NOT STATED

This last characteristic of prophetic material is perhaps the trickiest of them all. Sometimes it appears that God implies more than he says, and the people in the Old Testament picked up on that. Usually if prophecies have conditions, God states them clearly: "If you are willing and obedient, you will eat the good things of the land; but if you resist and rebel, you will be devoured by the sword" (Isaiah 1:19–20). That's clear.

At other times, it appears there is a general truth at play. The conditions stated by Isaiah above seem to apply even when God doesn't state them clearly. The prophet Jeremiah spelled out this idea when he said, "If at any time I announce that a nation or kingdom is to be uprooted, torn down and destroyed, and if that nation I warned repents of its evil, then

I will relent and not inflict on it the disaster I had planned. And if at another time I announce that a nation or kingdom is to be built up and planted, and if it does evil in my sight and does not obey me, then I will reconsider the good I had intended to do for it" (Jeremiah 18:7–10).

This truth seems to come into play at times in the Bible, even when it is not explicitly stated. For example, the prophet Jonah warned the Ninevites, "Forty more days and Nineveh will be overthrown" (Jonah 3:4). The prophet gives no conditions; he simply says that destruction will come. But as the story continues, the people of Nineveh repent and God spares them. Why? As the king of Nineveh said, "Who knows? God may yet relent and with compassion turn from his fierce anger so that we will not perish" (Jonah 3:9). He and the Ninevites seem to have counted on at least the possibility that God would turn from the prophesied judgment if they repented. And he did. King David appealed to this same idea when he said, "I fasted and wept. I thought, 'Who knows? The Lord may be gracious to me and let the child live'" (2 Samuel 12:22). These Ninevite and Israelite kings knew that God's judgments may have been conditional, even if not stated.

The Benefit—What Can We Learn From the Prophets?

So once we learn how to deal with prophetic material with its figurative poetry and ongoing fulfillments and the like, what can we learn from these ancient messages? After we do our best to learn the general and specific contexts for Isaiah, Jeremiah, and the other prophets, what do they have to say to us in our modern world? Over the years I have learned that multiple prophets communicate the following concepts, and I find that these points are highly relevant to us in our modern world.

1. God's plans are certain, but may be distant

If you work through the prophets within their chronological contexts, keeping Israel's subsequent history in view, you can see that God fulfills his purposes, even if it takes a long time. Some of God's prophecies came true immediately or within a short time. Others took years, even centuries. Some have yet to come true. But the many, many prophecies that have already been fulfilled show that God accomplishes his purposes, and the passing of even immense lengths of time is no deterrent. God's plans are certain and will happen.

This idea of certain but distant fulfillment sometimes discourages me. I want God to accomplish something *now,* or at least soon. God says that he will use everything for his purposes, and when something bad happens, I want God to fix it immediately or at least quickly. I don't want him to wait years before he acts, as I have sometimes seen him do. I especially don't want to wait for God's purposes that won't come true in my lifetime. Certainly God waits longer than one lifetime in some cases, as we see in the Bible. For example, God promised to give the land of Canaan to Abraham's descendants and then waited for some 500 years to do it. That's a long time. I don't want to live my entire life without God doing what he says he will do about the things concerning me. But as I read the prophets, I find that God often "delayed" his answer, and I don't doubt that God may well do the same for me or for you.

On the other hand, I also find it encouraging that God fulfills his purposes, regardless of time. It reminds me that

God is *way* bigger than me and my world. I'm concerned about my little part of the world in my little span of time, as I should be, but I need to be reminded that I serve a God with a *much* larger perspective. He will accomplish far, far more than I can see, do, or even imagine. I'm a small part of the big, long process of God working out his purposes in the world. I play only a small part, but I'm part of a big program that can't fail. I am on the winning team. This helps me want to do my part well.

2. God expects us to show faithfulness to him and to others

Just as God faithfully does his part to bring everything to its appointed end at the time he knows is best, so he expects us to do our part well. He expects us to be faithful to him and to others. This sounds easy in theory, but I find that my selfish, sinful inclinations often prod me to do things that gum up the works. Despite the challenges we face from within, from others, and from the world, we need to faithfully carry out what God has called us to do for him and for other people.

3. God calls us to be obedient

A big part of faithfully doing God's calling is obeying his commands, even if we don't understand them or we might suffer in the process. The prophet Hosea provides us with a perfect example. God called this man to marry a woman, and God told Hosea that she would be unfaithful to him in the future. So Hosea obeyed, and his wife ran off with other men. Then God called Hosea to take back his unfaithful wife and love her again. So Hosea obeyed. I can't imagine the challenge and pain that Hosea would have endured, but I see that he was obedient. And because Hosea was obedient, God used him and his family as a powerful example of how God loved the Israelites, even after they had been unfaithful. Although I don't expect God to ask me to do something as crazy as what Hosea did, I do find God asking me to do difficult things that sometimes cause me pain. Usually it's the pain of growth, as I surrender my selfish desires to act for the good of God and others. It helps me to remember that God always uses us when we obey. The prophets provide many good examples of obedient people in an earlier time, and we need to be obedient people in our day.

4. God is sovereign and will carry out his purposes

Although earlier parts of this chapter have touched on this idea in different ways, it's worth repeating. Perhaps the biggest theme woven through the prophets is that a great, sovereign God controls the nations and the flow of history, and he directs events so that his greater purposes come to pass. For the prophets, these purposes usually revolved around the nation of Israel. In our day that has changed, since the church includes people from around the world and is largely made up of Gentiles. Regardless, the sovereign God is still accomplishing his purposes and calls on his people to take part. As we are obedient, we help move that process along to its good end. If we are disobedient, we separate ourselves from what God is doing and can easily cause damage to ourselves and others. The prophets give us multiple examples of God's people who were obedient and thus were used by the sovereign God to do his will in their day.

Conclusion

So what on earth are the prophets talking about? Once we understand their context and learn the principles that help us deal with prophetic literature, we see that the prophets spoke loudly and colorfully to their day, as well as to ours. God is still God, and though some of his methods change, he is still in the business of fixing and blessing the world. The prophets still call us to obediently and faithfully do our part.

Next, let's deal with a related but rather distinct form of biblical literature—apocalyptic prophecy. This is where you find those weird visions in Revelation and the last half of Daniel. What on earth are they talking about? Actually, sometimes the visions aren't even *on* earth, and that's part of the problem. In apocalyptic prophecy, the prophets often use imagery not from this world, making apocalyptic literature extra difficult to understand. Apocalyptic visions are indeed difficult, but worth the effort because they are so vibrant and their messages so powerful. Let's turn and see how to handle apocalyptic prophecy and what nuggets those parts of the Bible have hidden for us in plain sight.

Study Questions

1. What do you make of the books of prophecy in the Bible? Can you identify with Martin Luther's description of the prophets given early in this chapter?

2. Do you find the figures of speech in the poetic parts of the prophetic books difficult to understand? Would

you agree that biblical poetry includes exaggeration to make a point?

3. According to this chapter, how did prophets function in ancient Israelite society?

4. Have you found a Bible study tool to help you bridge the gaps between our world and the world of the prophetic books—perhaps a tool like the introductions in a study Bible or the explanations in some other book like a Bible dictionary or Bible encyclopedia? If you have, what tool works best for you and why?

5. Were the following interpretive principles helpful to you? Why or why not?
    a. Prophetic writings may be figurative or expressed in contextual language.
    b. The chronology may be unclear.
    c. God's actions may be ongoing or thematic.
    d. God's judgments may be conditional, even if not stated.

6. Can you see how the prophets showed that God's plans are certain, even if distant? That God expects us to be obedient and to show faithfulness to him and to other people? That God is sovereign and will carry out his purposes in history?

9

Learning to Understand Apocalyptic Prophecy (at Least a Little)

The Problem—What's With Those Weird Visions in Revelation and the Second Half of Daniel?

In the last chapter, we addressed the challenge of understanding the biblical prophets—those spokesmen for God who preached in a distant context using lots of figurative language, and whose messages are sometimes difficult to understand. Now we turn to a related and perhaps even more challenging type of biblical literature—apocalyptic prophecy. As the second half of the name *apocalyptic prophecy* suggests, it *is* a kind of prophecy, so it's at least somewhat similar to the literature we discussed in the last chapter. But as the *first* half of the name suggests, this type of prophecy speaks about the apocalypse, or speaks about the future through apocalyptic prophecy. The terms *apocalyptic prophecy* and *apocalypse* may need some clarification.

Apocalyptic prophecy is another genre (a category or type) of biblical literature, and I think it's the hardest of all the biblical genres to understand. It's especially difficult because, for the most part, we don't have this kind of literature in our culture even though we have the other genres found in the Bible (history, poetry, laws, etc.). That naturally makes it harder to intuitively interpret when we do come across apocalyptic prophecy in the Bible.

We do seem to have a general understanding of what *apocalypse* means, at least as we use the term in our culture. When we say *apocalypse,* we usually mean the end of the world or the end of civilization due to some kind of disaster. Thus we may assume that biblical apocalyptic literature means something similar. But we may not know if modern and biblical apocalypses are the same, so we struggle when we come to apocalyptic literature in places like Daniel 7–12 and Revelation 4–22.

A student of mine named Joshua was studying Daniel and described this challenge by saying, "I had no clue what the second half of Daniel was about, and I didn't care to. The back half of Daniel is full of strange dreams and interpretations and prophecies that, at least then, didn't make a whole lot of sense. And reading it wasn't much fun since it always made me feel like I was reading a poorly written fantasy book where the author doesn't explain who the characters are. To me, the second half of Daniel was just one of those uninteresting parts in the Bible that you were allowed to skip, like the genealogy of Christ and the entire book of Numbers." Bingo! I think that describes it perfectly.

But Joshua followed those remarks by relating the pleasure of learning to understand this cryptic type of writing and the messages that God communicates through them: "Once you start digging deeper into the book of Daniel, you'll find that not only is it very intriguing (and entertaining!), but you'll also find that it is jam-packed with truth that is relevant for today."

I agree wholeheartedly with the second half of Joshua's statement as well. I used to despair when I came to the visions in Daniel, Revelation, and elsewhere. I tried to interpret them using the same basic principles I used with other biblical material—it's true, so I accept it as written, and try to understand it from my perspective—but those weird animals and numbers and such just seemed incomprehensible. Even after I had earned two degrees in Bible and theology, I still couldn't figure out most apocalyptic visions. Then I took a class on apocalyptic prophecy, and the professor began to teach us the characteristics of that genre. He also had us read a number of apocalyptic works from antiquity to familiarize us with its features, and he taught us some basic principles to interpret the apocalyptic prophecy in the Bible.

Once I understood the characteristics and guidelines for this seemingly foreign type of literature, things began to fall into place—well, most things. Suddenly those visions in Daniel and Revelation (and Zechariah, Ezekiel, and a few other places in the Bible) became far less mystifying and began to make sense. The parts referring to unnatural creatures and otherworldly beings shifted from making the visions incomprehensible to making them colorful and powerful. The elements that seemed to talk about the future (like the seventy "sevens" in Daniel 9) came into focus, though not entirely. Apocalyptic prophecy went from being my least favorite genre in the Bible to one that I enjoy immensely. It's vivid, compelling, and shows God's control even over very difficult situations. And as my student Joshua wrote earlier, it *is* jam-packed with truth that is relevant for today.

I now love apocalyptic prophecy, and many of my students have learned to appreciate it as well. The trick is learning to understand the features of apocalyptic literature and basic principles of how to interpret it. Let's discuss those now and see if we can use them to begin unraveling these strange and powerful visions. Hopefully you'll also learn to see how God used and continues to use apocalyptic prophecy to communicate what he is like, what he did and still does even in our modern world, and some of what he will do in the future at the end of this age. It's kind of fun, actually. Let's go!

The Description—What Are the Basic Characteristics of Apocalyptic Prophecy?

Most of us have a hard time understanding apocalyptic prophecy because those weird visions and dreams throw us off. Learning the basic characteristics of this very different type of literature helps immensely, so let's go over some of those now.

Apocalyptic prophecy states truth, but indirectly

When we are trying to understand literature from a distant culture, the more direct it is, the easier it is to understand. And most biblical literature is clear enough for us to understand without great difficulty. Even the type of prophecy that we discussed in the last chapter is easier to understand than apocalyptic prophecy, because with that kind of prophecy, God at least speaks directly much of the time. Often a prophet like Jeremiah will introduce a message with a statement like, "The word of the Lord came to me saying . . ." and go on to give the direct, true words of God. Though we may have to work to understand the context and some of the figures, the speech is mostly straightforward.

Apocalyptic prophecy is so different because it is *much less direct* though *no less true*. Actually, God communicates most of the same basic truths in apocalyptic prophecy as he does in "regular" prophecy, but in apocalyptic prophecy, he does so *very indirectly*. It's even more indirect than calling God a rock to communicate stability. An apocalyptic vision may portray God's stability and control by having a rock smash a statue and then grow (a rock that grows?!) to fill the world. That's harder to follow, but more fun when you get used to it. Apocalyptic prophecy is very different, very powerful, and very indirect.

Apocalyptic prophecy uses graphic, nonrealistic visions filled with strange elements

Apocalyptic prophecy communicates its messages through weird visions full of strange figures and symbols. In this kind of prophecy, God communicates through a prophet who may be called a "seer." *Seer* is one of the terms for a prophet in the Old Testament (1 Samuel 9:19; 2 Samuel 24:11). The term especially fits apocalyptic prophecy because there the prophet is *seeing* God's message in the form of a vision or dream rather than hearing it in words. The seer may see a vision when he is awake or a dream as he sleeps; it makes no difference. In apocalyptic prophecy, God communicates primarily through visions or dreams rather than through words.

These visions or dreams often contain things we don't typically find in normal life. Instead, they are filled with strange and colorful elements like angels and unnatural composite animals. These elements are often figures or symbols that stand for something else and the reader must first determine what the symbols represent before putting those elements together to get the message. This is challenging, but powerful and effective once you get the hang of it.

God used apocalyptic prophecy to encourage his people during times of persecution

God typically gave these strange visions filled with weird elements at times when God's people were undergoing severe persecution and needed encouragement. The stress and danger of persecution probably had them wondering what would happen and whether or not God could control their situation.

For example, God gave the visions in Daniel 7–12 to the prophet Daniel when the Israelites had been conquered and exiled by the Babylonians, and they must have wondered what the future held for them and if they would even survive. Some of the visions in Daniel 7–12 focused on what the Israelites were going through at that time (in the sixth century BC), and other visions spoke to events that would take place later in the second century BC. By then they would be back in Judea, but would experience persecution at the hand of a Greek king named Antiochus IV Epiphanes. Antiochus would kill tens of thousands of Jews and even try to wipe out Judaism, and God apparently gave those visions to show that he knew and controlled that dark period of history as well.

Much later, God gave the visions in Revelation to the seer John during the Roman persecution of the church during the first century AD. In each of these cases, God's people were facing difficult persecution and God used apocalyptic prophecy to encourage them. The apocalyptic visions showed that God knew and controlled the flow of history, including the persecution they were enduring.

Apocalyptic prophecy addresses evil around God's people

These times of persecution threatened to overpower God's people with evil. Thus apocalyptic prophecy addressed evil, as did other prophecy, but now the *source* of the evil had changed. Regular prophecy spoke mostly about evil and sin *in* God's people, so the solution was for them to repent and obey. In apocalyptic prophecy, the evil and sin were *around* God's people, so the solution was for them to *hang on* until God stepped in and did away with the evil.

In apocalyptic prophecy, God deals with evil personally

Both regular prophecy (like that in Isaiah or Jeremiah) and apocalyptic prophecy (like that in Daniel and Revelation) speak about God dealing with evil. Prophets like Isaiah warned the Israelites that they needed to repent of their sin or God would send human armies to judge them through conquest. In apocalyptic prophecy, God often promises to deal with the evil *around* his people by *personally* coming to wipe it out. Rather than using human agents, God would take care of it himself. We find the clearest illustration of this in Revelation 19, where the glorified Son of God comes on a white horse, leading the armies of heaven to wage war against the armies of earth. He crushes the enemy forces and casts their leaders into the lake of fire (19:20). Here and elsewhere in apocalyptic prophecy, God steps into history to personally deal with evil.

Apocalyptic prophecy focuses on the end of the world or the end of an age

Revelation 19 is one example of how apocalyptic prophecy looks to final solutions for evil at terminal points in history. For example, Revelation 19 describes God's judgment at the end of our current age. The earlier examples of biblical apocalyptic prophecy dealt with God's actions and judgment at the close of some other age. For example, the apocalyptic visions in Zechariah speak of God's acts to restore the Israelites after their return from Babylonian exile. The visions in Daniel 7–12 described God's work with Israel through the balance of ancient Near Eastern history. The visions in Daniel also address the intense persecution that the Jews would suffer during the period of Greek domination following the conquests of Alexander the Great. Though I don't fully understand how the Greek persecution in the second century BC, after Alexander, was "the end" as described in Daniel 8 (vv. 17, 19), that term does illustrate the apocalyptic focus on events at the end of an age.

Apocalyptic prophecy emphasizes God's control, even over terrible evil

As some of the preceding characteristics suggest, God gave apocalyptic visions to show how he was still controlling history, even during periods of persecution when evil powers and events threatened to overcome God's people. Perhaps you are like me and find that trusting in the control of a good God is much easier when we are experiencing good things in life. Then when bad things happen, like events that seem unnecessarily painful or senselessly evil, it's much harder to reconcile those with the idea of a good God running the show. Nonetheless, that's what the Bible teaches in general, and that's one of the main things that apocalyptic prophecy teaches in particular.

Our good God is sovereign and controls even the bad things. He knows that they will happen, he controls how long they will last, and he brings them to a proper end when he knows it is best—even if we don't understand. Apocalyptic prophecy emphasizes divine sovereignty over even terrible evil. I appreciate that emphasis, because sometimes life brings incredible pain, suffering, and even evil, and during those times I need to hold on to my trust in the control of a good God.

The Process—How Do We Interpret Apocalyptic Prophecy?

So once we get a general idea of what apocalyptic prophecy is like, how do we interpret it? How do we sort out the weird visions with their strange elements and figure out what they are saying? Actually, if we're asking these questions, we are already off to a good start. Once we know what apocalyptic prophecy is and can recognize it when we come across it in the Bible, we have already made good progress. The next thing is to learn some basic principles of interpretation that apply to this kind of literature.

Learn to expect figurative elements that stand for something else

Once we have recognized that we are dealing with apocalyptic prophecy, we need to become comfortable with the idea that this type of literature is *supposed* to have weird elements. It's *normal* for apocalyptic visions to include figurative or metaphorical elements that stand for something else. The visions are going to tell us truth but will do so indirectly through the figures.

Try to determine what the figures represent

Once we learn to expect figures or metaphorical elements in apocalyptic visions, what do we do with them? How do we know what they stand for?

Sometimes the vision itself will make the meaning of the figure clear. For example, in the visions recorded in Daniel 7 and 8, we read about a total of six beasts. In chapter 7, Daniel the seer sees four mostly unnatural composite beasts rising from a great sea. In chapter 8, he sees a ram and a goat, which are pretty natural except that the goat has only one horn (perhaps like a unicorn) that breaks off and is replaced by four horns. What do the six beasts stand for?

The visions themselves answer that question. In Daniel 7:17, Daniel asks some being who is present with him (quite possibly an angel) how he should understand what he has seen. The interpreter responds, "The four great beasts are four kingdoms that will rise from the earth." Clear enough. *Beast* equals *kingdom*. Then in chapter 8, after Daniel sees the ram and goat, the interpreter even tells him *which* kingdoms the ram and goat represent—the Medo-Persian Empire and the Greek Empire. Thus when the vision says the one (Greek) horn is broken and replaced by four horns, this obviously stands for Alexander the Great, who died and was succeeded by four Greek generals who divided his empire following his death. The beasts stand for kingdoms, not only in Daniel 7 and 8, but often in apocalyptic visions. Beasts representing kingdoms is one standard figure we find in apocalyptic literature.

Apocalyptic literature contains other standard figures as well. In Daniel 8, we can see that the goat's horns stood for the kings or powers that led that kingdom; heads in apocalyptic visions often mean the same thing. Even in our day, "head" often stands for authority, which it seems to mean in apocalyptic visions as well. Thus the heads of beasts in such visions typically stand for the authorities or leaders of various kingdoms. The more you read apocalyptic literature, the more you get used to such figures and the easier interpretation becomes.

Expect figurative use of numbers

Numbers make up an especially important type of figure in apocalyptic literature. In fact, frequent use of numbers is another characteristic of the apocalyptic genre. For example, if you think of numbers in the book of Revelation, you probably think of seven—seven churches, seven lampstands, seven angels, seven seals, etc. The book also has several sets of four (creatures, corners of the earth) and twelve (gates, tribes, angels).

But what do the numbers mean? Well, sometimes they are straightforward and literal. The four beasts of Daniel 7 stand for four ancient Near Eastern kingdoms (apparently, Babylon, Persia, Greece, and Rome). But *very often,* the numbers are *figurative.* Rather than representing an exact number, they represent a general idea. This is perhaps easiest to see with numbers like *seven* and *ten,* which the ancients thought of as full numbers. I find that in apocalyptic literature, *seven* and *ten* most often mean *all* or *full* rather than one more than six and one less than eleven. In addition to those full numbers, *one thousand* may simply mean a lot, and *three* may simply stand for a few.

Stick to the main ideas of the figures

Apocalyptic images are colorful and figurative, and we can easily get lost in the detail. We need to remember to keep it simple and look for the main idea. For example, what would be the main idea of an apocalyptic *beast* with *seven heads* and *ten horns* (Revelation 13:1)? If we understand that a beast means a kingdom, do we try to chase down how that kingdom had seven of one thing and ten of something else? If we remember that horns and heads represent power and authority, and full numbers like seven and ten stand for completeness, then the figure more likely represents a *kingdom* (beast) *with full power* (seven heads) *and full authority* (ten horns). Rome had full power and authority at the time of Revelation, perhaps somewhat like the United States does now. The main idea is that this kingdom has great power.

Using such an interpretive method can be challenging until you get used to dealing with the figures, but it makes more sense. God has more to say about powerful kingdoms than about impossibly shaped animals. The vision is communicating something that is true, but communicating it *indirectly* through figures. You just have to get used to thinking about what the figures *represent* rather than what they *are,* and then try to tie together the meanings of the figures to find the message of the whole vision.

Keep your options open as to how the vision will come true

Apocalyptic imagery tells what will happen and what God will do. The temptation is to interpret the images in a way that would make sense in our present world. If the vision were to come true during our time, perhaps such an interpretation would be correct. But if the vision isn't fulfilled until later, the form of the fulfillment may not be what we think it would be now. We need to keep our interpretations simple and general, and know that God will bring about the fulfillment in the way that is appropriate at the proper time.

For example, if a vision speaks of a future war with terrible weapons that cause great devastation, how should we interpret that? Devastating war is clear. Should we include in our interpretation weapons like conventional bombs, as we have known in past wars? Should we include nuclear weapons as we now have but rarely use? Should we include some type of weapon that will only be invented later? Any one of these might be correct, or none may be correct. If an apocalyptic vision says a devastating war will take place, then a devastating war will take place. The general idea is clear, but details may not be. We're better off keeping our interpretation to the basics and leaving God and the future to sort out the details. Apocalyptic visions give truth, but *in general terms*. We need to keep the options open regarding the details. We may overstate the interpretation of an apocalyptic vision when we read into it more than is appropriate for the genre.

The Benefit—What Does Apocalyptic Prophecy Teach Us?

Apocalyptic prophecy uses visions with figurative elements that tell us generally what will (or would) happen in the future. Depending on the age about which God was speaking, the visions may have already come true—like with the sequence of ancient Near Eastern kingdoms—or they may still come true in the future—like when the Antichrist will persecute God's people at the end of our age. Regardless of the time period involved, this literature emphasizes a few general, powerful ideas.

God is sovereign, even over evil events, and directs history to his desired end

Apocalyptic prophecy stresses God's control over even the worst things that happen. Many events in life are good for God's people; others are very bad. Either way, God is calling the shots, even if we can't understand how or why. Sometimes his sovereignty allows very bad things to happen, but eventually he uses them to bring history to the conclusion he desires. We may not understand it or live long enough to see it, but the Bible in general, and apocalyptic prophecy in particular, assure us that it is so. We need to remember this important part of the big picture. A good director is running the show, and the show will end on time and in the way his script says it should.

We are on the winning side, but we may well suffer casualties

Though I appreciate apocalyptic prophecy for its emphasis on God taking events to the right conclusion, I don't like how it allows for God's people to suffer along the way. I'd rather avoid the suffering, thank you very much, but the Bible doesn't always promise that. In the Old Testament, the Israelites often suffered as God carried history in the direction he wanted. In the New Testament, Jesus assured his followers that we would know trouble in this world, but that he would be the ultimate victor (John 16:33). The Bible teaches the same about the end of the world. God's side will win, but his people will not necessarily be exempt from pain, suffering, or even death.

Accepting pain and suffering is difficult for many people. We often try to avoid or lessen pain, and understandably so. Often we can succeed, but not always. Sometimes the painkillers aren't strong enough when sin or simple accidents inflict unavoidable pain. The Bible says that the world will get even more painful at the end, and both the good and bad people will suffer.

As I read the book of Revelation, I see suffering continuing, and believers suffering even death. I also see that God knows and controls this suffering and will allow it for a time. He will let many of his people suffer, but he will reward those who do. Ultimately he will end the evil and suffering, and take over in glorious victory. I like the idea of ultimate victory, but not the possibility of suffering along the way. I like that I will be on the winning team, but I must accept the fact that many of my teammates will suffer and some will die before God brings about the rightful end. Our side will win, but we may suffer. Ultimately that will be okay, because God will make sure that his team wins and his purposes prevail. It is a certain and sobering promise.

Conclusion

Understanding apocalyptic prophecy is tricky. It's different, indirect, and hard to intuitively interpret. It also has general characteristics that we need to understand and basic guidelines for interpreting it correctly. Once we learn these, this genre becomes less mysterious and quite dramatic and powerful. God uses it to show his knowledge and control of the future and his ultimate victory over evil. The message of God's sovereignty was important during the time of Daniel when Babylon had conquered the Jews, and during the time of the New Testament when the Roman Empire persecuted the church. It tells us today that God will direct events as our age moves toward its appointed end as well. God is sovereign and he will win, and so will we as we keep ourselves aligned to his purposes. Apocalyptic prophecy communicates that message in a vibrant, emphatic way.

Study Questions

1. Do you have trouble understanding apocalyptic prophecy like we find in Daniel 7–12 and Revelation 4–22?

2. Did the following characteristics given for apocalyptic prophecy make sense to you? Why or why not?
   a. Apocalyptic prophecy states truth, but often indirectly.
   b. It uses graphic, nonrealistic visions filled with strange elements.
   c. God used it to encourage his people during times of trouble.
   d. It speaks about evil *around* God's people rather than sin in them.

e. It often says that God will judge sin personally at the end of the age.

f. It emphasizes God's control, even over incredible evil.

3. Did the following guidelines for interpreting apocalyptic prophecy seem helpful to you? Why or why not?

a. Expect figurative elements that say one thing but stand for something else.

b. Try to determine what the figures represent.

c. Expect figurative use of numbers.

d. Stick to the main ideas of the figures, and keep your options open as to how they will come true.

10

Conclusion

What Have We Learned,
and Where Do We Go From Here?

What Have We Learned in This Book?

It's okay to be confused

You probably began reading this book because you know that reading the Bible is important, but honestly, you have a hard time understanding or getting much value out of some parts of it. I hope you feel that's okay. I imagine the vast majority, if not all, of the people who read the Bible would admit they feel that way at times. I imagine even teachers and scholars who study the Bible extensively would agree with that. I know I do. The Bible is God's inspired Word and he speaks through it and tells us lots of amazing stuff, but parts of it are simply difficult to understand and appreciate.

I hope that reading this book has also helped you understand *why* some parts of the Bible come across that way. As
God guided the authors of the Bible, they recorded what
God had done for them in the past, what God told them, and
some of how they wrestled with the challenges of life. All
that is good, but those writings all came from contexts far
removed from our own. The most recent parts of the Bible
were written about 2,000 years ago, and the other parts are
even older. Much of the world of those people was *very* different than ours, so reading literature from their world is
challenging at times. We're trying to bridge a great chasm of
time, distance, language, and culture when we read the Bible.
God helps us to understand the most important truths, but
the challenges remain.

On top of that, much of the Bible (the Old Testament
especially) was written when God was relating to his people
through a particular religious system with laws and rules that
applied directly to their system and nation. All that culminated in the life and ministry of Jesus, whose teaching, death,
and resurrection established a new framework for people to
relate to God. Believers today operate from within the new
framework, but much of the Bible was written under the
old one. That makes it harder to relate to much of what we
read. What from the old framework still applies to us after
the ministry of Jesus? What is still useful as an example? And
what may have little or no value to believers today given our
different world with our different framework for relating to
God? These issues often make parts of the Bible more challenging as well.

Although it's okay to be confused because of the distance
and changes from the original text to our world, God still does

speak through the Bible. Some parts are easier to understand, and some are more applicable. But even in the parts that are harder to appreciate, God usually speaks to us across the span of time and differences. He has hidden some truths in plain sight in the tough parts of the Bible, though some are harder to see than others.

The tough parts of the Bible still have important truths to teach us

In this book we have looked at the challenges of understanding and benefiting from a number of harder parts of the Bible: the laws of the Old Testament, the book of Leviticus, the long section of land boundaries in Joshua, the genealogies, the repetition of material in Kings and Chronicles, Ecclesiastes, the messages of the prophets, and finally, the cryptic visions in apocalyptic prophecy. We walked through the original contexts for those sections, what truths they would have taught to their original recipients, and what believers today can still learn from them. Let's do a quick review of each to solidify what we have already learned and help set the stage for how we can learn from other challenging parts of the Bible as well.

In the chapter about laws of the Old Testament, we discussed how legal material from one's own culture is not too interesting for most people, so the legal material from an ancient, distant culture might naturally be even less interesting. We are connected to the ancient Israelites as their spiritual descendants, but it's naturally difficult to understand and appreciate some of their laws. They were a different ethnic group (than those of us who are Gentiles) living in a different nation, and they related to God through their

165

national covenant, which is often called the Mosaic Covenant. The laws in that covenant taught and directed those people in that context, so those laws are often less clear and less relevant to modern believers who are Gentiles living in different nations, relating to God through the New Covenant established by Jesus. Despite these differences, God repeated some of the laws from the Mosaic Covenant in the New Covenant, so those repeated laws are directly relevant to us. Many of the other laws are still helpful to illustrate some of the qualities God expected from his people then and still expects now.

The chapter on Leviticus addressed that book's detailed descriptions of sacrifices, which clearly have been rendered obsolete by the sacrifice of Jesus, as well as the book's descriptions of feasts that most Gentiles don't celebrate. A detailed book on subjects of little or no relevance is a tough sell, but Leviticus does demonstrate some keys truths about God and how his people should relate to him. Leviticus clearly emphasizes God's holiness—his absolute moral purity and his separateness from us and our world. God is holy and expects the same from his people—but the Israelites of old weren't holy and neither are modern believers. Thus God made his people holy by covering their sin with sacrifice, and they needed to respond by living holy, obedient lives. Much of this is still true. The type of sacrifice necessary to make us holy has changed dramatically (Jesus instead of animals), but we still need to respond with pure lives. God hid some timeless truths (rather deeply, in my opinion) in this book.

Most of the latter half of Joshua describes the border divisions between the Israelite tribes when they lived in the land of Israel, making up what may be the least applicable part of the Bible for modern believers. Certainly the ancient Israelites needed good border descriptions, as all land deeds must be clear to prevent problems. Nonetheless, most modern believers aren't connected to the land of Israel, so any relevance to our situation is tougher to find. However, the book does demonstrate God's faithfulness in giving the land to the people of Israel as he promised, despite the centuries that had passed between promise and fulfillment. Likewise, God still keeps his promises, although he may again take centuries to do it. Waiting for something that we may never experience is tough, but as believers today we have an even better hope in many ways than did the ancient Israelites. Our hope is not for a land in which to live out this life, but a heavenly paradise in which to enjoy all eternity. Meanwhile, we don't relate to God through the Mosaic Covenant, but rather we enjoy a more direct connection to him through the New Covenant. And we benefit from God giving us the Holy Spirit as our comforter and guide during the journey.

Chapter 5, on genealogies, addresses these parts of the biblical story that use lists of names we probably can't pronounce and which belonged to people now long gone, most of whom we know nothing about. These records of who fathered whom seem quite disconnected from our world, and thus irrelevant. We discussed how these genealogies were far more meaningful for their original audiences. The lists recorded the Israelites' lines of ancestry, which helped clarify what rights and obligations these people had based on their place in society. We also noted how the authors of Scripture used genealogies to connect major characters in the stories, and highlighted certain teachings the authors wanted the audience to learn. Once again, the genealogies do contain some important truths, but they are often hidden rather well from the modern reader.

Our next chapter discusses the repetition of the history in Kings and Chronicles, which can appear pointless to the modern reader who may well read the books one right after the other. We noted that these two histories were apparently written for audiences separated from each other by at least a generation, and by the significant events of the Babylonian exile and subsequent return to Judea. These somewhat different audiences needed somewhat different messages, and the authors addressed those needs by shaping the same history differently. The author of Kings used the history of the Israelite monarchy to tell the exiled Israelites *why the exile occurred*—the nation had sinned, and God judged them justly. By contrast, the author of Chronicles rewrote that same history to those who had later returned from exile *to give hope for the future*. Even though the Israelites had sinned, God was restoring them, and their future would be challenging but ultimately glorious. The repetition of the historical material in these books with these meaningful differences served important purposes for the original audiences. They taught them (and remind us today) that our sovereign God is directing history as he knows best, and our part is to remain faithful to serve God's purposes in our place and time.

Chapter 7, on Ecclesiastes, seeks to explain the book's dark tone, showing that the author was speaking from his perspective and what we can learn from it today. Solomon, the probable author, wrote this negative work in part because he had a pre-Christian mindset and saw life as ending at the grave. From this limited vantage point, problems don't always get sorted out, and life often seems less than satisfying. Though the author repeatedly states in exaggerated poetic fashion that life is pointless or vain, it does allow us joys and pleasures in our work and relationships. And those that maintain a good relationship with God find added fulfillment in these when they are kept in their proper place (Ecclesiastes 12:13).

The chapter on prophecy notes that the prophets taught the same basic principles as Kings and Chronicles, which makes sense given that the prophets generally ministered during the latter part of the time period covered by these historical books. But unlike the historical narrative found in Kings and Chronicles, the prophets often spoke in poetic language, using many figures of speech that the modern reader may not understand. The prophets also spoke within historical and theological contexts that can be quite removed from our current situations. Thus the modern reader often must work hard to learn the historical context of the prophets as much as possible and interpret their messages in light of the Mosaic Covenant, through which the nation was relating to God at that time. Once we deal with these contexts appropriately, we see that God used the prophets to teach that he controls the events of history, both good and bad, and that his people are called to faithfully obey despite the challenges.

Our last chapter addressed the related but somewhat different prophetic literature called *apocalyptic prophecy*. Rather than speaking through the prophets' verbal messages, God communicated truths through the prophets' dreams or visions. These often include otherworldly and unnatural elements that can be difficult for us to grasp, but these visions taught largely the same truths as the more direct verbal messages. The visions spoke of the future and demonstrated that the God who controlled what Israel *had* gone through would also control what Israel *would* go through. Thus he had their future under control, though not everything in that future would be good. God allowed and used even the bad things for his purposes, which were ultimately good. These apocalyptic visions still communicate these same truths to us in our modern world. They should inspire confidence that God will make everything work out as he wishes—from whatever happens to us personally today all the way to what will happen to the world at the end of time. Our good God is running the show.

Where Do We Go From Here?

God is indeed directing history, and has hidden some great things in plain sight (or not so plain) in these challenging parts of the Bible. But where do we go from here? How can we learn from other difficult parts of the Bible as well? Can we come up with some basic guidelines that will help us deal with other confusing and seemingly irrelevant sections of the Bible? I believe the answer to that question is yes, though it may not be easy. The process involved in thorough Bible study requires some hard work. Fortunately, we have good tools to help us and God's Spirit to guide us. I offer the following principles, which I have found helpful in understanding God's Word, including the hard parts.

Learn the historical context of a passage as best you can

This is a basic but often overlooked step in interpreting the Bible correctly. I watch Christians approach God's Word by reading a passage, then immediately trying to interpret and apply it from our modern perspective without trying to understand it from the perspective of the original context.

As we have already noted, the biblical materials came out of a context that is usually very different than our own. It isn't *always* necessary to learn the original context to interpret a passage carefully, but it's safer, and often helpful.

As I mentioned in chapter 1, I find it helpful to ask the questions *Who? What? When? Where? Why?* and *How?*

> *Who—was the author? What do we know about him that is relevant to this book of the Bible?*
>
> *Who—were the original recipients? What about them is relevant to this book of the Bible?*
>
> *What—was the author communicating to his audience?*
>
> *When—did the events occur, and when was the book written?*
>
> *Where—did the events occur, and where was it written?*
>
> *Why—was this author writing this to this audience?*
>
> *How—did the author write what he did?*

I find that asking and answering these questions usually gets me reasonably close to the original context and often answers questions before they come up. Other times it helps to ask the right questions about what some part of the book means. To find this information, I typically go to a study aid, such as a study Bible that includes introductory material preceding each book. Bible dictionaries or Bible encyclopedias also have similar articles that help us to understand the historical context.

For example, before reading a book of the Bible, I ask myself the questions listed above. For some books, I'm familiar enough with them to remember much of the context. For other books, I may have read the information before but can't remember enough of it, or maybe I don't know it at all. In those cases, I turn to my study aid to review or learn more.

When I do read about the context of a book, such as Philippians, I see that the apostle Paul wrote the letter to the church at Philippi during the first century AD. I know a fair bit about Paul already, but I find it helpful to review that he wrote this positive letter from prison, of all places, and that he focused on encouraging this church, which he had founded some years earlier. This context helps me appreciate the tone of the letter, and I know I need to interpret what he says by first thinking about it from the perspective of an apostle writing to believers in a major city in the first century Roman world.

Interpret the passage in its literary context—immediate, book, and canon

After learning the historical context, we need to interpret the book in its proper literary context. This may sound more difficult than it actually is. It means that we need to understand a passage in the context of what the book says immediately before and after our passage, in the context of the overall message of the book, and in the context of the overall message of the Bible. In other words, we need to guide our interpretation by the context of a passage, and a passage won't mean something that doesn't fit its context.

Thus we should interpret the parts of Philippians in light of what Paul wrote immediately before and after that section, in light of the overall teaching of Philippians, and in light of what the Bible teaches as a whole. The proper interpretation of the passage needs to match or at least not disagree with these spheres of literary context.

I thought about interpreting Philippians properly a few weeks ago when I was running a marathon. I was running 26.2 miles through a beautiful part of Minnesota with over 6,000 other competitors. Along with the magnificent scenery, I enjoyed reading signs that people put up for us, as well as what some runners printed on the backs of their shirts. As I was approaching the twenty-mile mark and serious fatigue was setting in, I saw a sign that read MORTUARY AHEAD. LOOK ALIVE! It's hard to laugh after you have been running for three hours straight, but that sign did the trick.

I also read the backs of the shirts of runners in front of me at various parts of the race, and several proclaimed Philippians 4:13: I CAN DO ALL THINGS THROUGH CHRIST WHO STRENGTHENS ME. While I appreciated their boldness in advertising Scripture in a public setting, I wondered if they were interpreting the passage in context. I know the verse is true, but I find it a bit tricky to interpret. Does Christ give strength to run a marathon? Does he give strength to win a marathon? What does the verse mean in context, and does it apply to running marathons?

Similarly, I have also wondered about the proper interpretation of Isaiah 40:31 in relation to running: "Those who hope in the Lord will renew their strength. They will soar on wings like eagles; they will run and not grow weary." Again, although I know that the verse is true, I have found that hoping in the Lord with all my might doesn't keep me from getting weary when I run. What does such a passage mean in its proper context?

When we look at the context of Philippians 4:13, we see that the imprisoned apostle is speaking about being content no matter what the situation—regardless of how much or

173

little he has at the time. This fits well with the general context of the book, in which Paul encourages the Philippian believers in their Christian faith. It seems that in context, Paul is primarily saying that Christ helps him to be content in good and bad situations, and he obviously was in a difficult one at that time. I find the teaching to be challenging in a good way, but it doesn't seem to have much connection to marathons, although I would certainly describe the last six miles of a marathon as a bad situation. I liked the fact that people wore shirts proclaiming Philippians 4:13, but I think the verse best applies to *practicing contentment in life* regardless of circumstances.

Likewise, the context of Isaiah 40:31 seems to have little to do with running. The prophet Isaiah warned Israel that its sin would lead to God's judgment, but then promised that God would restore Israel after the judgment. Chapter 40 focuses on encouraging Israel at the beginning of the section focusing on restoration. The immediate context for the passage is that judged Israelites should take courage in God's power and plan for them despite the judgment they have experienced. The God who judged them will also restore them, and Isaiah uses the figures of birds flying and people running to portray people getting through challenges with God's help. Isaiah 40:31 is a great passage with helpful teaching, but it primarily addresses successfully working through challenges in life that are much greater than running.

Interpret by analyzing important words and grammatical structures

After learning the historical and literary contexts of a passage, we need to interpret its content. The author uses words and grammatical structures to communicate God's truth, so often it helps to analyze those.

Certain key words can be critical to correctly understanding a passage. For example, 1 Samuel 16:15 states that an evil spirit from God tormented the troubled and disobedient King Saul. What does the word *evil* mean here, and how can God be the origin of evil? These are common questions, and unfortunately a common response is to look up a word in a modern English dictionary. While this may prove helpful, it can also be misleading at times. Looking up a biblical term in a modern English dictionary assumes that the word means the same in modern English as it did when used in the Bible (at least as the translators of the Hebrew or Greek text used it). The meanings may be the same, or there may be enough difference to mislead us.

A modern English dictionary defines *evil* as "something seriously immoral or purposefully harmful." I agree that this is the way we most often use the term in our culture, and this definition fits the way the word is used in the Bible *much of the time*. But it doesn't fit the context of God's action in 1 Samuel 16:15. The author was not saying that God was doing something seriously immoral.

The better course would be to look up the meaning of a biblical word in a Bible dictionary based on Hebrew or Greek. Assuming that we can access and use such a tool (with some Bible dictionaries you don't need to know Hebrew or Greek), they are more likely to tell us what we need. Indeed, the dictionary of Hebrew words that I most often use lists a second major meaning for evil as "something harmful or unpleasant." I would describe this concept as "bad" rather than "evil," because many things in life are harmful or unpleasant without being immoral. This idea of *evil* meaning "harmful or unpleasant" fits the passage in 1 Samuel 16 much better. God did something unpleasant to Saul, but Saul likely deserved it. This example illustrates how looking up the meanings of key biblical words in a dictionary of biblical terms can help explain a passage and avoid potential misunderstandings.

Beyond the meanings of words, we also need to analyze the structure of *how* an author writes to better understand *what* he is saying. We do this intuitively, and thus we don't always do it thoughtfully. I find it very helpful to think through carefully the meanings of words, phrases, and sentences, as well as the connections between phrases and sentences. It helps me understand more clearly what the author is communicating, and ultimately, what God is saying. I find that when I do that kind of analysis it opens the door for God to speak to me clearly through his Word.

Assuming we want to analyze that carefully, how would we do it? We need to develop a method that works for us, but an effective methodology may well include several steps. First, analyze parts of speech (nouns, adjectives, verbs, prepositions, etc.) to understand how the *words* are functioning in a grouping of words. Then analyze groupings of words in phrases (prepositional, participial, etc.), clauses (independent, subordinate, etc.), and sentences, which make us think through how the groups of words are functioning by themselves and in relation to one another. We then link the groups (like sentences) into larger sections of the book, which helps us learn what each section says and how the sections fit together to form the overall message.

Next, we should test the validity of our interpretation. We do this by considering whether or not our understanding of a passage is consistent with the rest of the book and the whole of Scripture. If we think we have come up with a correct interpretation but it contradicts what God has clearly revealed elsewhere, we need to rethink our conclusion. It also helps to compare our conclusion with that of respected biblical scholars who have published their results in commentaries or other works. We should find that others agree with our conclusion. If not, again, we need to rethink our conclusion. It's always wise to practice humility, keeping open to the possibility that we may have erred. Hopefully though, we'll find that our interpretations line up with the rest of Scripture and the conclusions others have reached.

As I noted earlier, the process of interpreting the Bible well often requires much work, and some people are better at it than others. But the more we do it, the more clearly we will understand what various passages and books of the Bible are saying. When we go through the process of uncovering those meanings in light of the original context of the book, we are more likely to understand what the original author was saying to the original audience, which is how we know what the Word of God says.

Figure out if and how the teaching of a passage applies to our modern setting

After we have learned the historical and literary contexts of a passage and interpreted that passage at the levels of words, groupings of words, and in sections, we should have uncovered what God and the author were saying to the original audience. But how do we take the messages for ancient biblical audiences and determine if and how they apply to our modern world? Again, the process includes a few key principles.

177

First of all, we need to try to determine if a biblical text teaches a timeless principle that transcends culture. If we find it repeated in Scripture and not cancelled by later scriptural teaching, then we may have a timeless principle. Loving God and our fellow humans, and not stealing or committing murder, are clear examples of timeless principles.

Sometimes, though, a text expresses a teaching specific to a certain culture, for example, expressing love with a holy kiss or asking slaves to show proper obedience to their masters. In these kinds of cases, we need to extract the principle and apply it to our culture in ways that are appropriate.

Beyond principles that are timeless and those tied to specific cultural practices, sometimes we find biblical texts that record some act specific to a particular situation, or that deal with something superseded by later revelation. These kinds of texts have little or no modern application. Examples might be David's moving Israel's capital from Hebron to Jerusalem, or Paul's asking Timothy to bring his cloak when he comes again. Such activities were obviously limited to a singular context.

If we determine that we have either a timeless principle or a truth that can be transferred appropriately to our culture, then we need to apply it. The text may be a command, principle, example, or promise, and God can speak through each of them to instruct, guide, illustrate, and encourage his people today and throughout time.

Conclusion

God has told us some things quite directly in his Word, and others he has hidden in plain sight. Sometimes it takes some effort to hear what God is saying, and sometimes it requires extra work to uncover the truths he has embedded in the tougher parts of the Bible. Moreover, it takes a willing heart to follow through and obey the truth we have learned. But as we discover and obey God's Word, God directs and blesses us with fruitful lives and the promise of a rich eternity.

Study Questions

1. Did the following guidelines for interpreting the Bible seem helpful to you? Why or why not?
   a. Learn the historical context of a passage.
   b. Interpret the passage in its literary context—immediate, book, and entire Bible.
   c. Analyze important words.
   d. Analyze the structure of what the author says.
   e. Figure out if and how the teaching of a passage applies to our modern setting.

2. Have you found a Bible study tool to help you bridge the gap between our world and the biblical world, one that gives you help with interpreting the Bible (a study Bible or some other resource like a Bible dictionary)? If not, might it be worth investing in such a resource?

Things I Love About Each of the Books Most People Skip

Below is a list of the books of the Bible many people consider difficult or even boring along with one or two things I love about each. As you read through these books on your own, keep an eye out for some of the wonderful things they teach us about God and about ourselves.

Leviticus

- Although it's easy to get lost in the details of sacrifices and festivals that most of us don't practice, Leviticus shows God's concern for holiness. God is morally pure and wants his people to be morally pure whether they lived before or after the ministry of Jesus.
- Leviticus describes the sacrifices and gifts the ancient Israelites were to offer to God. The sacrifices and gifts Christians present to God today will differ dramatically from those described in

Leviticus, but we should still give God our best and in ways that cost us something.

Numbers

- I love how easy it is to relate to the Israelites in this book. Even though they were seeing God's amazing miracles firsthand (daily manna, for one), still they continually rebelled against God. How often do we forget to express our love for God even with all the blessings in our lives?
- If it weren't for God's constant provision, the Israelites would not have survived. We often see the Old Testament God as a God of harsh judgment. But his fatherly love toward his people is evident in one provision after another throughout the book of Numbers. Even his judgments are for their own good.

Deuteronomy

- Notice how often the original audience of this book was commanded to *remember* the good and bad from their earlier time in the wilderness. For us today, *remember* often simply means to think about something again, but in this part of the Bible the word meant to think about something *and act accordingly.* The Israelites needed to remember their past mistakes *and not repeat them,* and remember how God had taken care of them *so that they would remain faithful to him.* We would do well to keep in mind what we have done and what God has done in the past to help us remain faithful as well.

Ecclesiastes

- Although this author seems to be having a very bad day, he rightly points out that so many things in life (pleasures, relationships, material possessions) promise great satisfaction but don't always deliver. He also notes that those things may be good and are to be enjoyed as long as we maintain a good relationship with God as our foundation.

- This book also reminds us how important it is to occasionally take a step back from the daily press of life to think about the big questions. *What is really important in life? Am I too concerned about things that won't really last? Since most things won't last, am I focused on the most important things?*

Isaiah

- This book contains some of the most spectacular prophecies in the entire Bible—the role of the Persian king Cyrus in restoring God's people to their homeland, Jesus' virgin birth, and Jesus' suffering. God described these things in great detail centuries before they happened. This reminds us of how God *knows* and *controls* the events of the world and in our lives. God's knowledge and control are sometimes hard to see, so we can take comfort in such clear illustrations of those truths in the Bible. If God knew the difficulties Jesus would go through many centuries in advance, he must know the difficulties we go through as well, and he can make sure they work out for good.

Jeremiah

- Jeremiah is a person we can both have compassion for and admire. He was a sensitive person who suffered greatly—rejected by friends and family as well as enemies, beaten, imprisoned multiple times, and called a traitor. God didn't allow him to marry or have children. He obeyed God's calling even though it meant frequent suffering, plus having to say difficult things at difficult times to mostly hardhearted people. We can admire his courage and obedience in the face of great difficulty and in spite of how it must have hurt him. Jeremiah is a great role model when God asks us to do something we find challenging.

Lamentations

- The author of Lamentations was feeling down—for good reason. He had just witnessed the destruction of Jerusalem and Israel's temple at the hands of pagans. In the book, he confesses that the Israelites deserved this harsh punishment and that God ultimately was the one who made it happen. But in the very heart of the book (3:21–26), the author reminds himself of God's faithfulness. He knew that the faithful God who punished Israel as he had promised would also be faithful to restore Israel as he had promised. Likewise, when we have sinned and suffer for it, we can be confident that God will faithfully bring good out of our situation as we confess our mistakes and yield ourselves to him.

Ezekiel

- Ezekiel was an Israelite priest who was exiled to Babylon when God punished Israel for her unfaithfulness, and God revealed some amazing truths to him. One of the most striking is the vision of God abandoning the temple back in Jerusalem (chapter 10) and thus withdrawing his presence from this sacred place. This truth must have been terribly difficult for a priest to comprehend, but it demonstrated that God is willing to abandon things we hold sacred when those things no longer fulfill his purposes. Might not God do the same in our day, choosing to withdraw his blessing from some institutions or organizations that we hold sacred and move on to others in order to fulfill his purposes?

Daniel

- Like Ezekiel, Daniel was exiled to Babylon. Daniel had probably been born and raised in Jerusalem and would have expected to live out his life there. But God had other plans, and Daniel was taken far from home and thrust into a very different, pagan, and unwelcome situation. Nevertheless, Daniel served God (and his pagan overlords!) faithfully in this new place, and God clearly blessed him there. Likewise, we may end up in situations not to our liking or choosing, but we need to remain faithful regardless and trust that God will bless us.

- The book of Daniel includes a number of dreams. In the first half of the book, Daniel received training as a court advisor, education which probably included dream interpretation. In addition to that training, God also gave Daniel extra ability to interpret dreams, which he used when the regular court advisors couldn't interpret the king's dreams. Then in the second half of the book, Daniel has dreams and visions that even he can't interpret! God used Daniel to interpret one kind of dream at one time, and then gave him different dreams at another time that he couldn't understand—even with angelic help! God has his purposes and may do different things at different times that catch even godly people off guard.

Hosea

- Here's another good guy to whom God gave a really tough job. God told Hosea to marry a woman that he warned would be unfaithful to him, and it happened just that way. Apparently through no fault of his own, Hosea had to endure and work through the pain and challenge of an unfaithful partner. That's really tough—but perhaps no less tough than God having to endure an unfaithful partner in Israel. God was the perfect lover, but his people rejected him to pursue other gods. Although Christians today aren't under the same national covenant with

God that Israel was, we should still be committed to our faithful divine Lover. When we choose to act faithlessly and chase some other pleasure or desire, are we acting like an unfaithful spouse toward God?

Joel

- This book is about bugs—lots of bugs—hungry bugs that ate crops. For a nation of mostly farmers, lots of hungry bugs are really bad news. A plague of locusts had apparently devastated Israel, and God used that disaster to warn his people that things could get even worse. He could (and later did) bring enemy soldiers to devastate the land and cause even more damage than the locusts had. Unfortunately, the Israelites didn't listen to Joel's warning and paid a high price for their hardheartedness. Likewise, God may tell us that we are off track in some way in our lives, and warn us to set things right lest we cause greater damage. If we remain hardhearted and don't change, we might also end up in a much worse situation.

Amos

- Amos was apparently just a regular guy. He was a farmer with crops and animals when God called him to minister as a prophet. Amos knew he didn't have the usual credentials and training. When he was challenged by an established religious leader, he demonstrated his commitment to do whatever God asked of him (7:12–17). Credentials and training are not bad things, but they also aren't always necessary to be used by God. Sometimes availability and willingness are more important than credentials and training. Are you available and willing to do whatever God asks of you?

Obadiah

- This book is about God making things right—eventually. Jerusalem has just been sacked, and the nearby related people, called the Edomites, thought that was great because they could profit. Israel's loss was their gain, but Obadiah told them that God would restore Israel and settle the score. The Edomites had built their capitol on a high, easily defended site, but God promised to bring them down anyway. And he did exactly that, but it took *centuries* for the events to play out. God's promises are certain, but he may take a *very* long time to fulfill them. Are you okay with serving a God who does the right thing in the right way at the right time—even if it doesn't match up with the way and time you think things should happen?

Micah

- Micah promised that God would restore his people after judgment—but it would turn out to be a *really* long time after judgment and in a way his people wouldn't expect. Micah prophesied that God would first judge Israel, but later restore them. He would restore them, in part, through a leader who would be born in Bethlehem (5:2). That leader, of course, was Jesus, and God would indeed use Jesus to restore Israel, though at a time and in a way they probably didn't expect. Micah ministered some time around 700 BC. God judged Israel in 586 BC and began restoring them several decades later. Notice that Jesus didn't minister until about *600 years* later (who wants to wait that long?) and restored Israel spiritually rather than physically, as they probably wanted and expected. Can you accept that when you ask God to work in certain ways, he may just take much longer than you wanted and answer your prayer in a very different way than you expected?

187

Nahum

- Nahum promised Israel that God would finally give them relief from a big problem. The mighty, cruel nation of Assyria had been a power in the region for centuries and had ruled Israel and its neighbors with an iron fist for more than one hundred years. Now God was promising deliverance. Could it really happen? Now? Perhaps it seemed unlikely, like some distant dream that could never come true. Nineveh was large and well defended by strong walls, rivers, and a moat—seemingly impenetrable. But it did fall. In 612 BC, two armies combined to attack and conquer the city, apparently aided by a flood that had helped erode its defenses. The unthinkable happened, and God delivered Israel from Assyria, just as he promised. Do you have any problems that seem insoluble or bad situations that seem to have existed forever and that you think will never go away? Do you trust that God can fix even those situations?

Habakkuk

- Habakkuk was sure God had a bad idea. The prophet was troubled by all the sin he saw in his society, so he pled with God to do something about it. In response, God promised he would, but in a way that Habakkuk thought wrong. God said he would take care of the sinful Judeans by judging them with the army of Babylon. Habakkuk couldn't believe it. Judah was bad, but the Babylonians were even worse! Why would God punish evil people by using people even more evil? Wasn't that a bad idea? But God assured Habakkuk that he would judge the Babylonians as well—years later, at the proper time. By the end of the book, Habakkuk accepts that God knows what he's doing and trusts him to do what is right. Have you ever asked God to do something in a situation, only to see him do something you thought made it even worse? If God is *really* sovereign and good, can you trust him to do what he knows is right, even if it might seem like a bad idea to you at the time?

Zephaniah

- In Zephaniah's day, Israel was looking forward to "the day of the Lord," the time when God would step into history and make things right. The Israelites had been having difficulties and assumed that when God made things right, he would bring down their enemies and elevate them instead. Zephaniah surprised his fellow countrymen and pointed out that God would indeed make things right, but would actually begin with the Israelites (who were doing a number of things that weren't as they should be). They didn't want to hear that, but God knew what was best. Might you be in a similar situation? Maybe you think God needs to step up and take care of some people who are doing bad things to you, when God may actually want *you* to deal with some of your own issues first. Might you have a few planks in your eye that need removing? (Matthew 7:3–5).

Haggai

- The Israelites needed a wake-up call. They had been exiled and later returned to their land as God began to restore them as he promised he would. But then they had more to do than they could get done—reestablish their homes, get society functioning again, and rebuild their temple as their place of worship. They had made a good start on the temple, but then money got tight, other priorities pressed in, and their work on the temple ceased. God used Haggai to give them a prophetic wake-up call—rebuking them for not completing the job and encouraging them to get it done. Guess what? They actually did what the prophet told them to do! If you read through the prophets, you will see how unusual that was. Typically God's people didn't obey so quickly. Are you like that? Has God spoken to you about doing certain things, but other matters keep crowding them out? If so, can you reverse course and do what you need to do without God having to give you a serious wake-up call?

Zechariah

• Zechariah is probably one of the hardest books in the whole Bible to understand. It begins with a number of *apocalyptic visions*—prophetic material that uses mostly unrealistic imagery to communicate theological truths. At the time of Zechariah, people probably understood such imagery much better than we do now, so the prophet's audience may have had little difficulty understanding what he said. God was telling the Israelites how he would help them in the future, in part through Jesus and his ministries. Note how Zechariah 9:9 describes something from Jesus' first ministry (Matthew 21:5), and the very next verse (9:10) tells about something that Jesus will do when he returns. Just as surely as Jesus entered Jerusalem on a donkey when he came the first time, so will he bring peace to the earth when he comes back. I don't know when that will be, but won't it be glorious?

Malachi

• "Go ahead, try me!" says God. The Israelites in Malachi's day who had returned from exile had struggled to rebuild their nation and were discouraged at how poorly it had gone. Most were still quite poor, and life was hard. God had promised renewed glory to Israel, but the faithful Israelites were still waiting for that to become a reality. Was it really worth doing what God asked? In response, God encouraged those Israelites to remain faithful and promised that those who trusted him would indeed be rewarded. Do you ever feel like the Israelites in Malachi's time? Like you've been faithful but things are hard and it's just not worth it? Maybe you need to continue to hang in there, and trust that God will bless you in due time.

Revelation

- Is God really in control or not? Well, yes and no. The Bible often argues that God is in control, but our experience on earth sometimes suggests otherwise. The book of Revelation addresses this matter of God's sovereignty. Even though it is often difficult to understand, Revelation shows that God is both *in control,* and *not quite.* The book alternates between scenes in heaven and on earth. The heavenly scenes shows God's perfect control *there,* whereas the scenes on earth often reflect chaos and evil, with God's control *eventually* taking over. As Christians we know that we will eventually experience life under God's perfect control in heaven, plus Revelation teaches us that God will eventually manifest that same control here on earth.

- What will heaven be like? Even though Revelation includes a number of scenes in heaven, it's a bit tough to sort out what heaven will be like exactly. That's partly because Revelation is largely written in apocalyptic prophecy, which is rich in figurative visions that communicate truth in non-literal ways. So what will heaven be like? Many details are unclear, but one thing is perfectly clear (as described in Revelation 4). God will be present in his awesome, complete glory, and all creatures will bow in frequent, reverent worship of the true, sovereign God. That is our end—living forever in the presence of the almighty God, and it will be absolutely glorious! Our journey may well be bumpy at times, but our destiny will make it all worthwhile! Hallelujah!

Dr. Boyd Seevers is professor of Old Testament studies at Northwestern College in St. Paul, Minnesota. He received his PhD from Trinity Evangelical Divinity School and his ThM from Dallas Theological Seminary. Dr. Seevers studied and lived in Israel for eight years. He has presented papers at numerous national conferences and has published more than one hundred articles. Boyd and his wife, Karen, live near Minneapolis, Minnesota, with their four children.